. . . . LOUIS BRAILLE

Louis Braille was three years old when he was blinded, and if it had not been for the devotion and kindness of his parents and friends, he would have become an outcast and beggar. Despite his blindness, he was determined to help himself and others like him, and constantly experimented with a system of punched dots that would enable the blind to read. But he could not combat official resistance to his revolutionary innovation, and his unique method remained unrecognized during his lifetime. Now, a century later, long deserved recognition is given the man whose method of printing, writing and musical notation for the blind is known in every country and is used in every language.

LOUIS BRAILLE

WINDOWS FOR THE BLIND

by J. ALVIN KUGELMASS

Decorations by Edgard Cirlin

JULIAN MESSNER   NEW YORK

To my wife, Elizabeth

· ·

. . . . . ; . . . . AUTHOR'S NOTE

VERY SPARSE ARE THE PUBLISHED MENTIONS OF BRAILLE'S
life. Older libraries, museums where some were housed, fell
more easily to wars. Some mention of him was found in the
reports of the Royal Society of France at the Bibliotheque
Nationale, in Paris. There are some few mentions in social
studies on the blind, published in the XIXth Century, at
the British Museum, London; the National Library, Brussels;
and in Rotterdam, Frankfurt, Berlin, Vienna, Stockholm
and Marseilles.

The tiny village of Coupvray, Braille's birthplace, un-
changed and untouched after 150 years despite several in-
vasions, provided atmospheric background. The saddler's
shop still stands, as well as the little hollowed step leading
to it where the blind genius sat as a child. Two peasants,
descendants of Braille's cousins, afforded halting anecdotes
which have been handed down. Horny-handed men, easier
with a plow than with words, they told somewhat of his parents, tales told them by their grandparents.

The great libraries in the United States have little. The
Division for the Blind, Library of Congress, has nothing.
The head braillist there, herself blind, confesses sadly that
no research is available in this country. "I wish I could see
just for a year so that I may delve into European libraries,"
she says desperately. "A life on him is needed so very badly."

There were scanty mentions also in—

*Trente Ans d'Etude et de Propagande en Faveur des
Aveugles.* Publisher: Jules Meshin, Paris, 1908.

Des Sourds: Muet des Aveugles, by Hubert—M. E. Vallerous. Publisher: Victor Masson, 1853.

Ueber den Unterricht der Blinden, von August Zeune. Berlin, 1849.

Royal Commission of the Blind, Deaf, and Dumb Reports. Publishers: Eyre & Spottiswoode, London, 1889.

From Homer to Helen Keller, by Dr. Richard Slayton, Publication, American Foundation for the Blind.

It is difficult to think of a XIXth Century giant, of Braille's stature and impress, who has not come under the scrutiny of our practicing biographers. Men of far less consequence, of less universal appeal, have been pedestaled on the biographical shelves. Yet no biographer, before this undertaking, troubled to illume the life of him who strove so agonizingly in his search for light.

The contemporary biographer is as much of a reporter as he is a pale-handed scholar. He is perhaps a geometrician in that given two points, he can sedulously plot a third. In Braille's case, the plotting was a chore under a microscope. For he faced me a century away, dim, elusive and baffling.

The pioneer in biography has little need for apology. He can but reassemble, as best he might, the elements which come to hand to form a three-dimensional being. Where elements are missing, unlike a Supreme Being, he cannot fashion them. He can but make do so long as he does so with humility and dedication.

I feel no shame in confessing to a bowed head when I stood before his bust with the blinded eyes, in the village of Coupvray. Reverence is due this Prometheus of the blind for even as I write this, untold millions are paying him homage as with their fingertips they touch the light he brought.

. . . . *CONTENTS*

I Darkness at Dawn

THE LITTLE BOY LOUIS, WITH THE BROWN, SPARKLING
eyes was playing in his father's pungent-smelling workshop.
As his father swung the broad, shining knife, thick shards of
leather slapped down on the floor beside him. Sometimes, the
thick slices were like half moons. Other times, they were
beautiful triangles. Mostly though, they were just unhappy-
looking slabs with no shape at all.

Louis tried fitting them together. He was three, so form,
substance and light had great meaning and interest. That
was very important, the fitting of a triangular piece of
leather against a square. When the sides fitted snugly together, the boy was quite delighted.

The nondescript shapes appealed to him, too. Through

the dim vision of a child, they were endowed with magic. By cocking his head to one side, he could see faces and houses and trees—the things of familiar meaning to him. He could sit in the sunlit doorway and let his imagination go where it would.

His father, a giant of a man, the saddle maker of the village of Coupvray, not many kilometers from Paris, was very tender with the little one. He carved out horses, cows, people, dogs and even a little Christ from the bits of leather. His son had a collection of toys which was the envy of all the little ones in the village.

At noon, from the house across the cobbled yard, Mrs. Braille called them for lunch. Big Louis and Little Louis, as they were known, walked hand-in-hand across the yard to join her at the ceremonious lunch that is the way of the French.

After lunch, Big Louis and Little Louis napped and then they resumed their work, the big one at making saddles and reins for the thriving agricultural community, the little one at peopling his imagination with things of greater consequence.

"My son will never be a saddle maker," Big Louis said throwing him high in the air. "He will be a priest or a professor."

Big Louis was greatly respected in his village. He was not only a thrifty man, but he was a devout one. He was kind to his wife Constance, and he maintained a warm dignity with his neighbors. Twice, he was named to the village council, and once he succeeded in raising a fund for a new church bell. He was thus as much a man of parts as one can be in a simple little village.

Constance Braille, his wife, came from a hamlet hard by, and so she did not show so many of the airs and fancies which, for example, were the lot of the butcher with his Parisian wife.

"True, my husband is far from bankruptcy," she would say. "But we are simple people and I am a farm girl."

Often the village curé came by and talked with Big Louis about local problems. He regarded Little Louis with a kind and favorable eye. "That one there is endowed with an inner life. See how he can play for hours by himself. It is a rich imagination that one there has."

One day, not long after Little Louis's third birthday, in the year 1812, the great blow fell.

As usual, he was playing in his father's shop. Marie, the daughter of a neighbor, wanted to take Little Louis to the near-by village pond.

"The day is cloudy," Big Louis told Marie kindly, "and my son will take cold if he wades. We will let him play here."

That very day, he had promised the local advocate new reins for his horse. The advocate had stopped by early in the morning while the family was at breakfast to remind Big Louis that he was to go to Paris on an inheritance case.

"I beg of you, my friend," the lawyer said, "my reins look bedraggled. They break at every turn in the road and they certainly will not make me look fashionable in Paris. I should greatly appreciate the reins, at the very latest, this evening."

"You will have them," the saddle maker said. "I myself will deliver them to your house by this evening."

Little Louis had settled himself in the comfortable little hollow in the doorstep which was worn by the footsteps of scores of years. His father was trimming the reins, dipping them in his brine solution, kneading them in his hands, stretching them across the loops on the beams of his ceiling.

Little Louis, holding one of his leather strips against the sky, saw his father's face in the leather's contour. Only the thick curly hair was missing. He was gravely disappointed.

"Look, father!" he cried. "Look, father. Here you are in your own leather. Look, father."

His father answered absent-mindedly. Louis squinted at the contour of his bit of leather and smiled to himself. He would soon put hair on the wondrous shape. He went to the ancient bench where his father worked and took one of the small awls with which the reins were pierced to form the buckle-holds. Then he began to hack at the edge of his shard of leather. He put it on the floor and scraped away with the very sharp point. But the tough leather would not give.

His father was on top of the rude bench tugging away at the reins tightening them as much as possible before winding them about spools. Thus, as a result of straining at them and catching the strain they would not shrink so much when they got wet.

Little Louis held up his bit of leather and squinted again to see if the hair was formed. It was not quite right. He held the bit of leather close to his face with the awl close to his eyes like an artist measuring a perspective. Then he drove hard with the awl. The sharp instrument glanced across the tough leather and went into his left eye.

He screamed. His father jumped from the rude bench and came rushing to his side.

"Son, son!" he cried, seeing the blood, but he did not think there was anything seriously wrong. Little Louis had scratched himself so very often.

Then he looked again and cried in horror.

He grabbed the child and ran across the cobbled yard shouting "Constance, Constance." Mrs. Braille appeared at the window of the one-storied house.

"Louis," she screamed, frightened at the sight. "Louis. what is it? My God, what is it?"

"His eye," the big one shouted hoarsely. "His eye."

Constance cast a kerchief over her head, tied the knot and came running, the while praying to the Virgin.

Big Louis, still holding the child, managed somehow to

mount his horse. He helped Constance up behind him and they galloped across the fields to the house of the veterinarian, the only doctor in the little town.

The greatest despair of Dr. Horace Duclos's life was that he was merely a veterinarian. He studied a great deal and read medical reports not only on horses and cows but on men as well.

"Let us see, let us see," he murmured to the distraught parents. "Let us see. Perhaps nothing much is injured. The eye is a formidable organ though it appears very delicate. We shall see."

He tried to stanch the flow of blood and it was many hours before examination was possible. Finally, when the flood subsided, he turned to the parents. The afternoon had come and gone. No one had eaten. The little boy was very pale lying on the couch whimpering softly, and great, convulsive sobs shook his little body. A black patch had been put across the injured eye.

"What can I tell you, my friends?" the horse doctor asked. "What can I tell you? I know nothing. I know only about animals. But I fear the worst. I fear the optic nerve is destroyed." He went on. "If I am wrong—and because I know nothing, I am sure I am wrong—his other eye may be good. One eye has little to do with its mate. That much, I do know. Wait a few days and we shall see," he counseled.

With the boy in his arms, and Constance walking alongside, his father rode slowly home.

They undressed the little boy and put him to bed. Big Louis rode over to tell the advocate that his reins would not be finished in time.

"That is nothing, Louis," the lawyer said. "I have heard the news. Come with me to Paris tomorrow, if you will, and we will see a doctor friend of mine who attends at Napoleon's court. With my influence, he may agree to have a look at the little one."

The next morning, Constance packed a lunch for her husband, her son and the advocate, and away they trotted to Paris behind two black horses.

By nightfall, they reached the gates of the city, crossed the *Pont-Neuf* and quartered down in an inn.

The next day, Big Louis waited outside the great, ugly court building till the advocate was through pleading his case and then they went to see the famous Dr. Armand Fontaine.

The little boy had refused to eat and he was ashen-gray and deathly looking. His lips were bloodless and he was still in great pain. Both his eyes were now covered with a silk kerchief, for he had complained that the right eye ached him too.

The waiting room was crowded with the great from the court and with officers from Napoleon's armies. Evening had almost fallen when they were finally admitted to the examination rooms of Dr. Fontaine.

"What have we here? A small one? Tsk, tsk. It is nothing.

These small ones always recover."

But when the kerchief was removed, Dr. Fontaine was very grave. "There is nothing here to work with. There is nothing, my friend," he said to Big Louis. "Only God can grow another eye. I have nothing here to work with," he repeated.

The other eye was also closed. "Have you pain, little one?" the great man asked.

Little Louis nodded. The doctor pushed back the lid with a merciful thumb while an assistant held aloft a torch that was covered with a tallow. The eyeball looked into the flame stolidly, frozen, unblinking. He held a mirror before the uninjured eye. "What do you see, my little friend?" he asked. Little Louis was mute.

"Come, come what do you see?"

"Rien, monsieur," the little one said.

"Black, is it then?" the doctor mumbled to himself. He flickered the torch again, stroked the hair of Little Louis and turned to Big Louis.

"I fear, but I cannot say as yet. I fear both optic nerves are destroyed. You are not one of my rich patients whom I will cozen and deceive. You are the friend of my friend. I admit most brokenly that surgery of the eye is but little known. We are more skilled in treating flesh wounds caused on the field of battle than any other ailment," he said sadly.

"This little skill and knowledge we have of the human being has been obtained solely through trial and error and from victims of war. We know how to amputate a leg and how to treat a bullet wound in the flesh. But we have little skill with other things. I can tell you straight out, my friend, that an eye injury remains an injury. If it heals, we bless the good Lord. If it does not heal, we continue to bless Him."

Big Louis looked brokenly at the doctor. "What can we do? What can I do? I will pay anything," he pleaded.

"It is not that," the doctor said kindly. "It is not payment that will do it. Trust in the Lord. That is all I can say. I frankly admit I can do nothing. Wait two or three weeks and we shall see whether the right eye heals. The left eye is gone. That I can tell you honestly."

Big Louis took his son back to Coupvray. All the long way through the fields he murmured to the little one. Some instinct told him to describe the wayside.

"There is a bird perched on top of the tree," he told his son who sat mutely in the saddle in front of the tall father. "The bird is looking for his wife. Hear how he calls."

The boy heard dimly. The pain was still very great. Tears rolled down his cheeks and his father said sadly to himself: "The fault is mine. Mine the fault. I shall never forgive myself."

When they got to the house, he was still crooning to his son. "Here is our house. There is the pond shining in the sun. There is the shop. Soon I will make you wonderful toys."

Constance came running from the whitewashed house.

Smoke was coming out of the chimney, and there was the wonderful smell of a roast in the air. She had prepared a joyous homecoming.

"What news, what news, what did the doctor say?" she asked. Her face blanched as the big man slowly shook his head.

"Not before the little one," Big Louis said warningly. "Not before the little one."

Constance threw the apron over her head and ran into the house crying: "Why could it not have been me? Holy Virgin, why could it not have been me?"

During the next days, the pain slowly left the little boy. Neighbors came to visit, brought him little sweet cakes and jams. The curé brought a bottle of his best wine.

"It is strengthening, this wine. It will give him back the blood he has lost. It will invigorate him," the curé said.

He sat down on Little Louis's bed and talked with him for a while. Louis managed a smile and sipped some of the wine.

"See, he is better already," the curé shouted. "My wine and the Holy Virgin will work wonders," he exclaimed.

Even Big Louis took heart when Little Louis smiled. "Look, he smiles!" he shouted to Constance. "See, he is better."

In a week though, they knew. The little boy was blind. He would never see again.

"Do not despair," said the advocate. "Do not despair,"

said the curé. "Do not despair," said the village school-teacher. "Sight has been recovered before and he is young," they all said.

But the weeks passed and Little Louis got stronger and better and his eye healed, but he could not see.

Then Big Louis, a man of reality, a man who knew when things were ordered by God, set to work whittling a cane. Little Louis was blind. A cane was needed.

II The Clouds Gather

ALL THROUGH HIS CHILDHOOD, LOUIS BRAILLE NEVER AS-
sociated wind on his face, the warm sunlight on his head,
the sound of birds, all the outdoors, without the incessant
tap-tapping of his cane.

As he grew older, his cane grew with him. For as his body
grew, Big Louis, now prematurely whitened, whittled him
another cane.

Once at confession, Big Louis wept to the priest. "This is
my curse, that is my cross. Each six months, I need a reminder
of my sin when I must whittle a new cane for my growing
son."

"Your son is blessed that he has parents so devoted," the
curé said gravely. "It is the will of God," he said sternly to

Constance when she came and wept. "God does not wish you to cry so much. It is not seemly."

Little Louis grew easily accustomed to his life of darkness. Now and then, he would get a blazing streak of pain across his eyes. Now and then, he would recall the shape of a tree, the look of a cloud as it scudded rapidly across the sky, the silhouette of the hills near his home as they ranged to form a valley, his father's face, the look of his little dormer room.

But by the time he was seven, as he wrote later, these remembrances of form, shadow and light were soon merged into feeling and contours of his own creation.

"What is color?" he questioned later in life. "There is no answer. That is what I mean by remembrances of my early childhood. I know what is meant by color but I cannot see it inside of me. I know surely there is such a thing as color but it is an elusiveness I am forever pursuing."

Each morning at eight, his father took him by the hand and led him across the rise in the hill, across the crest of the road to the one-room schoolhouse.

"How strikes you the weather today, Little Louis?" he asked the quiet boy tap-tapping along the frost-hardened road. "What will be the weather today?"

"There is a softness to the wind, father," Louis answered. "I scent a dampness in it. There should be rain. Tell me how the sky looks."

In the schoolroom he was given the first seat on the first

bench. The schoolmaster confessed his inability to understand how Louis grasped arithmetic and such geography as was taught at the time.

"He leans forward in his seat and listens acutely. You can see his mind assimilate, grasp. Then he leans back and sorts. You can see him sorting in his mind."

Those were fatalistic days. The world was not cruel; it was merely indifferent and the afflicted were considered accursed by God. The hardy and the well of spirit were hard put to make do, and the rest? Well, the rest could fend their ways.

The Church spoke of the will of God; the government shrugged its shoulders, and the afflicted did as best they could. The lame became beggars. The insane were considered a nuisance and the government refused to feel any responsibility to any but the strong. Men were beginning to question whether this should be so but these doubts were lost in the louder noise made by almost constant warfare.

For that reason, the Brailles resolved to safeguard Louis's future as well as they could.

"He will need everything we have," they agreed. And Father Braille bent himself to the task of storing monies while Mother Braille became thriftier than ever. They tried to lay aside as much as they could for the little blinded one. "He will need much when we are gone," they said.

The villagers were kind. "There comes *petit* Louis," they said when they heard the tapping of the little cane.

They scratched out grooves on the road so that he could follow a straight path to the school. They indented the road to the pond so that with his cane he could find his way and sit in the sun listening to his playmates.

Tap, tap, tap, his stick went down the road. So many taps to the big tree. So many more to the pond. That many more to the left, to his aunt's house.

His eyes were at his cane's end, but as he explained later, it was the tapping that stayed with him, the theory of tapping that was to mean so much to the world later on.

Sometimes, friends his own age came to play with him. But he sensed their embarrassment when they formed games in which he could not join. He sensed, too, that soon they would forget all about him. He followed their cries and the way they chased one another up and down the near-by hills. He tried to imagine himself playing hide-and-go-seek but all he could do was act as mediator for them.

His face showed his early maturity. There was kindness before there was need for it and there was a kind of parenthetical score about his mouth even before there was need for experience to form lines on his face. His body was thin and his face was pale.

He became a great friend of the curé and would talk to him for hours about the old biblical tales.

"Your son is destined," the curé told his father. "He is destined for something that I cannot foresee. I swear to you, I see a pattern in his life. See now, how his friends defer to him even while they forget him. See how he sits, the cane between his legs, and calls out encouragement to them. He is needed somewhere. There is a mercy from God in all this."

His mother, however, saw nothing but the small wasted body. "I have but one son and he will not be long with me," she said. "He coughs. He is thin. He is blind. No, I am wrong. He is blinded," she added bitterly.

At thirty, both his parents were very aged. They could not do enough for him. He would remonstrate with them at dinner. "I am very comfortable. I like being blind. I like being alone with myself."

Sometimes his maturity frightened them. "He is only nine and he speaks with the curé of things we never heard about," they told their neighbors. "Where will he go when we are gone? What will he do? Who will care for him?"

Louis went for long walks by himself. He cast himself down, feeling the earth, caressing the moss against a tree.

Sometimes he pummeled his poor eyes and cried out, "No, no! Truly, no."

The good Dr. Duclos tried to explain to the parents.

"You must remember that he was not born blind. He blinded himself. The shock is great and may even last all his lifetime. I have seen horses who were blinded by a fire or some accident. They canter across a field, they rub their faces in straw, they suddenly turn about as though something is behind them. They are destroyed simply because they are not understood and there is the fact too that they are useless.

"All his life, your son will behave like one of my poor patients, my horses. All his life, he will seek his lost vision.

"I am a poor horse doctor. But I do know that the loss of a sense is not easily accepted. Your son behaves differently because he is different. Always, always, he will seek sight."

His parents did not understand him. They did not know how to cope with their sightless, brilliant son. He seemed to father them, to chide them when they worried about him.

"You work too hard, Father," young Louis would say about five o'clock in the afternoon. "Stop working. Let us come and walk in the fields."

Big Louis cast off his leathern apron, and walked with his son. His sense of guilt about the accident of long ago never left him. He tried to accede to every whim, tried to predetermine every want of his intense blinded son.

And how he tried to understand him! He walked with young Louis for hours, hearing him comment on things that were outside his scope. He answered him as best he could, about the physical components of life outside the blinded eyes. Without comprehension, he grew very close to the boy, and learned to understand, if dimly, that his son had a scholarly and introspective bent.

Often he went to the priest and tried to work out his bewilderment by talking.

"He is so poetical, Father. He seems to speak of things I do not know about. Is he sad?" he once asked desperately. "Is it that he is sad? Is that why he speaks in such a far-off manner?"

The curé smoked for a while on his clay pipe. "It is not for us to understand. Let him go his own way. If he feels things about him that you do not comprehend, it is not your business. Do what you can as a father; leave the rest to God. His salvation will be worked out. Be patient. Let him find his way. He is young."

He puffed some more. "God always works in strange ways. Who knows? I cannot advise you. You have been a fine father and your wife a splendid mother. That is all God asks of you. What more can you ask of yourself?"

In those days, a blind person did not attend school, as a rule, and was usually trained as a professional beggar. In many cases, in Europe and Asia, the blind were cast out of the household at an early age as accursed. Or they were hired out for some menial task as a beast of burden.

In most cases, the blind person was sold to a manufactory where he shoveled coal his livelong day and slept on the ground or swept piles of fertilizers for those who handled the commodity.

There were no set rules for the blinded, but it was understood they were outside humanity, could perform no money-gaining function and were set aside as human culls.

The American and French revolutions, which were to

spread the feeling of brotherliness among men, and which had recently taken place, had not yet made their impact felt.

Many blind persons earned a meager living by forming into bands of mummers. They strolled from town to town across Europe and mocked at their own afflictions and made people laugh. People laughed not because they were crueler than they are today. They just had not been taught that a handicap was to be pitied and the handicapped person helped. Governments had not yet been taught that, either.

It was, for example, the custom for fairs to include a troupe of blind persons who performed as a silent orchestra. Each blind person wore a pointed hat. The leader, or conductor, would swing a stump of a broomstick at a sheet of music, while the rest of the blind cast would puff cheeks or saw with sticks at stringless violins.

Passers-by would toss coins when the conductor beat his troupe with his stick. The whole thing would be conducted with a ghastly solemnity and the effect of the silent, blinded orchestra would move the people to merriment.

It was not vicious. It was just that there was no way of integrating the blind person into the economy, of working out a way for him to earn a living. In most households, where everyone had to produce some way of earning money, his was an extra mouth to feed, and usually there was not enough for those able and well. So, most blind people became professional beggars.

Many died of starvation and the cold. The Paris gendarmerie and the police of big European cities each morning found scores of helpless persons dead of cold or hunger. It was routine and not considered merciless. There just was no place for the blind person. There just was nothing he could do.

When Louis was ten, he asked to be enrolled in a special school for the blind at Paris.

"Whoever heard of a blind child going to school? Are you mad?" his father asked him. "Are you mad?

"You will not be a beggar," the elder Braille said proudly. "We are putting aside funds for you and perhaps the curé will help you find some post in the church. But of what use is a school to a blind man? What kind of a school is this? This is madness."

But Louis was not mad. The advocate had told him of the special school. It was there that the children of the nobility went, and blind relatives of the new, rich bourgeoisie.

"Father," he burst out. "Father, I beg of you. The blind are the loneliest people in the world. Father, here I can distinguish one bird from another by its call; I can know the entrance to the house by the lintel. But am I never to know what lies beyond the confines of my hearing and my feeling with my hands? Only books can free the blind."

"But, my son, there are no books for the blind," Big Louis said with bewilderment.

"There are, there are," the boy cried. "In the school in

Paris there are books for the blind. Monsieur the advocate has told me there are books."

Big Louis spoke with the advocate. It was all true. True, the books were ridiculous, but at the school in Paris the blind children of the fortunate of the world did have books, such as they were.

"What else is there for your son? Why not?" the advocate asked sternly. "You can afford it."

At that time, relatives of nobility who were struck blind by disease or accident, were usually given minor pensions with which to eke out a simple life. They were not considered marriageable; they were just organisms who happened to have relatives rich enough to care for them.

There seemed little reason, then, to instruct the sightless in reading and writing when even the well, for the most part, could not read or write. So even the rich did not think it necessary to have the sightless instructed.

The school in Paris which young Louis wished to attend was the *Institute Nationale des Jeunes Aveugles.* The National Institute for the Young Blind. Not that there was anything like a national institute for the old blind. Not by any means.

The school had been founded by an unsung pioneer, one Valentin Haüy, back in 1784. Haüy, the heir to a large fortune, and apparently a person of great sensitivity, had been much distressed by the sight of a blind, soundless band performing at one of the Balkan fairs. He vowed to devote his life to the blind. He inquired into the matter and discovered that the blind were skillful with their fingers, very receptive to music, and his compassion knew no bounds.

In 1780, he wrote his mother that he was going to spend both his fortune and his life improving the lot of the blind.

"I am aware of a lack of humanity on the part of the humanists," he wrote. "Here we have the spectacle of thousands of people, unfortunate enough to be deprived of just one of their senses, and sentenced to the lot of people who are bereft of all of their senses." He was referring to the vicious ways in which the insane were handled.

"There is here a great waste. I shall try to redeem this waste."

Haüy was then a young man and looked upon as an eccentric when he founded his school and obtained a charter from the French government.

It wasn't much of a school even as schools were then known. About twelve students were registered. They lived in the cramped quarters in the old section of Paris where Haüy had purchased a ramshackle building. He had no instructors to start with and made the mistake of enlisting persons employed at the local "madhouse" to care for his few unfortunates.

One day he came upon one of his staff beating one of his blind charges, and soon decided to take a personal hand in running the school. His friends scoffed at him but he re-

mained true to his vow. He moved into his school, shared the
food and lodgings with his pupils and began to pay attention
to the mode of instruction. The once gay, young Parisian
became a social visionary.

His first syllabus was a pathetic affair, a thing he himself
admitted.

"Even if my students are trained to read and write, what
shall they do later on?" he asked himself.

He answered his own question and set down the theme of
his own personal mercy: "I cannot care what they do later
on. If only I have been enabled to erect an avenue for them
into the life about them, my work will have been done."
And then, he said wisely, "Someone will take up from there."

At first, the method of instruction was cumbersome and
heartbreaking. Out of painfully fashioned twigs, letters of
the alphabet were formed. Along these rude twigs, some as
many as six inches high, the students learned the twenty-six
letters of the alphabet.

Haüy cut out the twigs, fashioned the letters. Then he
took a simple sentence, such as: "My name is Valentin Haüy,"
and constructed an entire sentence. The sentence was mounted
on an easel-like frame stretching across the poor, shabby
schoolroom and the students clumsily felt their way, eking
out a letter, piecing out a word.

Haüy, more of a promoter and a social service worker
than a schoolmaster, brought his rich friends to the school
and got them to contribute to its upkeep. They watched the

students tap their way to the front of the room and actually spell out the sentence. Their amazement knew no bounds. "This is an incredible affair," they told Haüy. "Simply amazing," they said, smelling their scented pomander balls against the violent scents from the kitchen hard by.

In government circles, Haüy was looked upon as a troublemaker, as one of the newer products of the French Revolution who wanted abrupt changes. "He wants to go against God," a beadle in charge of a band of blind persons remarked. "He is anti-God," he said. "Of what use is it to teach the blind how to read?"

Soon the scoffers discovered that the blind at the Institute could read only from the twigs Haüy constructed. "There are no books for the blind. Will Haüy construct books of twigs for the blind? This is ridiculous."

But the twig method for teaching the blind did not long survive the founding of the school.

One day, one of Haüy's students, who also acted as doorkeeper, was given a card by a friend of Haüy. "Tell him I have called," the friend said haughtily.

The blind student clutched the card closely so that he would not lose it. When Haüy came to the school very late in the night, the student was waiting for him.

"A friend called, Master," the student said. "Here is his card."

Haüy dismissed him with a kind word but the student followed him to his room.

"Master," he said, "have you felt the card?"

"What do you mean?" Haüy asked kindly.

"Please do not think I am impertinent," the student said, stammering, "but the card is embossed and I felt the edges. Perhaps sight reading can be made from embossing," the young man said haltingly. "This is what I mean . . ."

But Haüy needed no instruction. He sensed the idea. As he said later: "It needed but a place where those concerned with their problem could foregather. The problem would be uttermost and thus the problem could be solved."

And so, not long before Louis Braille was entered into the school, embossing of books for the blind came into being. The new method revolutionized the course of instruction. Here was a method by which letters could be brought down to almost normal reading size. True, the embossed letters were an inch high, and there were not only whole sentences, but entire paragraphs.

Haüy arranged for movable type to be cast in great letters, about as big as the newspaper headlines of today. The type was deeply etched, so it would bite hard into soft paper. On the other side of the paper, there would come up a fixed impression and the students would thus be taught to read a letter at a time.

Within two years, the Institute had a semblance of a library. There were exactly three books. Each book was divided into twenty parts. Each part weighed close to twenty pounds. The cost was enormous. But Haüy spared no expense.

His school was now a real school. There were books of instruction. His enrollment rose to twenty pupils. They could learn to read, but of course could not write.

It was to this school that Louis Braille came in his country homespun, with his shabby trunk, the one used by his mother when she came from her village to wed his father.

Big Louis carried in the trunk, shook hands with Valentin Haüy and delivered his pale, sightless son.

"I beg of you . . ." the big man said haltingly to Haüy. "I beg of you . . . He is a sensitive boy. I beg of you . . ."

Haüy grasped him by the hand. "You have nothing to fear. We will do our best."

The other students helped Louis carry his trunk to the second floor. They shook hands all around.

After a dinner of beans and porridge, Louis was escorted by his sightless new friends to his bed. It was not like his own dormer room at Coupvray, but he knew he was home. All about him, there were sightless such as he.

"I have come home," he said smilingly to Haüy.

He did not sleep well, he told him in later years. He did not know exactly where he was, where to go to make his toilet, where his clothes were. The little room was cold and cheerless. The sounds of Paris traffic came up to him, the strange sounds of wheels striking against the cobbles. He could hear the hoofbeats of horses. His life came to him in syllables of sounds. His ears were all. Only sound was important to him.

There was smell, there was touch, there was taste, but upper-most was sound. He was to learn to understand touch and to transform it into windows for the blind but not until he had endured great agony and defeat—most of it at the Institute to which he came as a small, frightened, lonely, blind boy

III The Finger Moves

LOUIS TOOK UP HIS NEW LIFE AWAY FROM HOME WITH the aplomb of a much older boy. The new student speedily became popular with his blind brothers, most of whom were Paris-born. He taught them country lore while they, in turn, told him undreamed-of things about city life. The pale boy, wracked by an incessant cough that was to kill him at an early age, felt as though he had come into his own.

"There was a feeling of coming home," he wrote later. "I was with people similarly afflicted and there was none of the halting embarrassment with which the seeing regard us. I was with my brothers," he said simply.

His day was an exciting one after the limited routine at home. It was a healthier atmosphere for him, too. He was not a person apart and could indulge in the same activities enjoyed by his classmates.

The tuition and board were free to those unable to afford it. The older Braille, when asked whether he could afford 75 francs a month for Louis's keep and instruction, had offered to pay more.

"Perhaps there is one here who has no relatives to help him. I should like to help," Big Louis said clumsily. "I am only a poor saddle maker as wealth goes, but we have none other but this one," he said, stroking his son's jet-black hair. The sightless face of the younger one looked up at Big Louis with great pride.

But Haüy refused offers of help and convinced Braille that his son would be well treated and invited him to come to Paris as often as he wished and visit at the school.

The school dined at dawn on very simple fare, and each morning, after breakfast, the odd students assembled in the classroom which was a well-like affair similar to operating theaters in hospitals.

They ranged themselves in circular rows, one loftier than the next. The instructor was in the pit.

The instructor clapped his hands, and in came two servants bearing the gigantic books now printed in the embossing method. They were tremendous affairs and were mounted on great platforms.

The elementary students, such as Louis, were coached in the alphabet. Then, the advanced students were taken in little groups later in the afternoon. But all assembled in the same classroom. The school, as was true of all schools at the time, was run with military precision.

The servants, who were mostly recruited from the Parisian dregs, were not too kind to the blind students. They stole what they could of dainty tidbits brought to the students by friends or relatives.

The second day, while Louis was in his little bare, cell-like room he heard a soft footstep on the threshold. He heard someone fumbling with his hamper of clothes. Louis was too terrified to call out or say anything and soon the footsteps went away.

A cold roast chicken and a great pastry his mother had prepared for him were gone. He was never to forget the theft. It was his first contact with the outer world, away from the muscular and gentle protection of his father and his soft, tender mother.

"I knew then that the blind are prey to anyone who wishes to prey on them. That they are helpless," he wrote when he was fourteen years old. "Perhaps the blind should teach the world the compassion it lacks," he added in a letter to the curé.

The world was indeed lacking in compassion, he discovered when he went on forays with classmates.

He had early formed a friendship with a boy some two years older than he. This lad, Jean d'Anjou, a distant relative of the noble d'Anjou family, was given the chore of helping the new boy become acclimated. Jean had been blinded by a fall at the age of nine. His mother, a socialite and a Parisian beauty, soon regarded him as a burden and gratefully accepted Haüy's offer to place him at the Institute.

Jean was especially taken up with Louis, when the newcomer asked him to describe his face.

Jean said, "I have curly hair. I have an unfortunate nose. Here, feel. . . ." Louis felt.

"It is an unfortunate nose," Louis agreed.

"I am somewhat rich. I have brown eyes, as I remember. I have a mole on my cheek. Most of the d'Anjou family have moles. Here, feel. . . ."

Louis felt. "It is a most distinguished mole." The boys giggled and became warm friends on the spot.

The third day Louis was at the school, Jean invited him for a walk.

"I can find my way about the street and come back like a homing pigeon," he said.

Taking Louis by the hand, he led him out into the noisy thoroughfare. Louis was terrified within his darkness, without the strong hand of his father beside him. Jean was about three inches taller and walked with a surety that was the envy of the provincial lad.

Jean chatted easily. "To the left is a fine bakery. When your father comes, you must take him in there and get the glaced cakes. They are very good. Unfortunately, I am all out of them."

Louis said, "But I have some francs my father has given me. Let us get some now."

It was a great adventure for the boy to walk into a shop, his hand tightly clutched by his new friend, and ask in a firm voice for the glaced cakes.

"Do you wish the pink or the blue?" a female voice said.

"Let us have both," Louis said proffering a handful of coins.

"That is enough," he heard the woman say, her hands discarding coins in his hands, selecting the ones she wished. "That is enough. I would not cheat a *pauvre* blind one."

Louis was to hear that phrase most of his life—"I would not cheat a pauvre blind one." He winced but said nothing.

Hand in hand, they walked out of the shop. As Louis descended the little step from the shop, he felt a thud on the back of his head, then a shrill jeer. The paper sack was snatched from his hand, and then he felt a thud against his coat. He placed his hand to his coat and felt something warm and sticky.

He smelled his hand. It was a familiar barnyard smell. "What is this? What is this?" he heard Jean saying over and over.

They were surrounded by scores of mocking, shouting youngsters.

The two blind ones tried to walk on, but they were halted by blows.

"Beggars, beggars!" their tormenters shouted. "You have begged cakes."

Jean firmly took Louis's hand and turned back to the school. At that moment, Haüy came running along.

"My blind ones!" he shouted. "Get away!" he screamed at the gamins. "Get away, you spawns of the devil."

"Do not fear," he said to the trembling Louis. "Do not fear. They do not understand. Perhaps the world will grow up some day."

He led them back to the school, chatted with them, soothed them and left.

An embarrassment fell over the two boys. Finally, Jean said, "That's the way it will be for us always."

"No," Louis shouted. "No!"

"What do you mean?" Jean asked.

"I don't know," Louis said. "I don't know. But are we animals? This could never happen in Coupvray," he said bitterly.

He soon learned more of the anguish of being blind. One evening, at the second of the two meals of the day, as he sat next to Jean, he heard the ladle sound in his soup dish, immersed his spoon but felt nothing. His spoon merely sounded and pinged against the porcelain.

He muttered to Jean. "They have given me no soup."

"It is those villains of servants again," Jean said. "We must speak to Monsieur Haüy. Have some of mine."

· 45 ·

"No, thanks," Louis said. "I am not hungry."

He crept from his place, tapped his way up the steps, and threw himself on his bed. Sleep did not come to him that night.

The next day, he tried the street again, sought out the kind bakery woman, and asked her to write a letter for him. Fortunately she could write a bit.

My *chèr* Papa: I beg of you to take me home. I am unhappy here. The blind are animals to the Parisians. I am hungry. I am cold. The servants rob me. Just today, I was set upon and pelted by Paris gamins. They threw dung upon me. Father, please come and take me home. I will not be much of a care to you. Please take me home.

But for the fact that the post then was not as it is today, the history of the blind would be different. Louis's letter to his father did not arrive for ten days or more. In the meantime, he learned to accept insults, theft, blows and sneers. He learned very rapidly that his place was at the school among his own kind.

When his father—good, faithful Big Louis—came galloping, his face drawn and his eyes fearful, young Louis had already adapted himself and was quite composed.

"It is true, Father, that I would be sheltered with you and cared for. But my place is here simply because books are here. I am truly happy here." He had almost forgotten his misery.

Big Louis returned to Coupvray, his heart heavy within him and again sought out the priest.

"I beg you again to let him find his own way," the curé said. "Let him do what he wishes. He is a child, but older than we are in suffering. Let him be," he added sternly.

The boy was an apt pupil. Soon he was helping the embosser who had been told to turn out the first book of the Bible in the embossing method.

" 'Let There Be Light,' " Louis repeated softly when the first, huge clumsy pages were struck off. "That is a good phrase for us to remember," he told Jean.

One day Louis chided Haüy for translating only childish writings into the embossing method.

"Monsieur," he said firmly, "I am now eleven years old. I am not interested in the tale of Reynaud the Fox any longer. Reynaud is very fashionable with the younger set. How about some more advanced reading?"

Haüy threw back his head and laughed.

"We shall see. We shall see," he promised. "I am buying embossing presses of my own and the cost will be cheaper. We can then print almost anything we wish. First, however," he added, "I wish there were some way of teaching you to write, no matter how awkwardly."

For weeks thereafter, Louis thought about ways. He kept

his own counsel, did not confide in Haüy or in Jean. He again sought out the bakery woman and wrote to his father. About a month later, a mysterious package arrived for Louis Braille.

Trembling with excitement, Louis went to his room, unwrapped the package, and set to work.

A few hours later, he came tapping his way to Haüy's chambers and rapped diffidently on the door.

"May I disturb you for a moment, Master?" the pale boy asked. "Please do not laugh at me," he begged, and held out the paper in which the package had been wrapped.

"Is it all right, Master?" he begged again.

Haüy tenderly stroked the wan face. "You are a good boy," he said absent-mindedly. "I am very proud of you."

Louis had asked his father to send him the alphabet cut in bits of thick leather. Big Louis had enlisted the aid of the curé, who in turn set the local school children to work with sharp little knives.

Knowing the alphabet by feel, Louis had merely traced along the contours of the letters and managed to make his first bold strokes at writing, thus:

"My name is Louis Braille."

"You must come and meet a woman friend of mine," Haüy said to him some days later. "I will take you on a little holiday."

True to his promise, the next day, he told Louis to dress

in his best—a velvet suit his mother had made for him from an old dress.

Arrayed in striking blue, Louis was taken in a coach to meet the woman who was to have not only a profound effect on his own life, but incidentally, and more importantly, over the blind of all time to come.

Louis was ushered into a great room. He felt soft carpets under his feet. He was aware of the size of the room by the distance from which he heard a sweet voice welcome him.

"This, then, is the revolutionary you have told me about?" he heard a woman say. He also heard, to his consternation, the muffled thump of a cane.

Soon the sounds of the cane drew nearer and a soft, fragrant-smelling hand was exploring his face.

"This is the lean face of a poet. He shall make much trouble, this one," he heard the musical voice say.

"Come, sit with me," she commanded.

He could feel satin as she led him to the couch. A small enameled box was placed in his hands. "Sweet comfits for you," she said.

Haüy discreetly sat himself on a small chair near by. "Why do you wish advanced reading?" the woman asked him.

"I am no longer a child," he said with embarrassment. He leaned forward. "I pray you, do not be annoyed with me, but I heard a cane . . ."

"Yes, I am blind, too," he heard her say. She felt for his face and kissed him on the brow. He smelled her perfume and on her cool hand he could feel great gems.

"Do you know who I am?" she asked in a slightly mocking tone.

"No, madame, I do not," he said. Then boldly: "But I do know you are blind, too, and a very great lady."

"Sit quietly, and I shall tell you something in my own language," she said.

He sat quietly and heard the rustle of her gown. Then he heard a burst of golden music in the great room. There was a ripple of keys and then another great burst. The music came fleetingly then burst forth again in noble chords and swept along triumphantly. Then hauntingly, there came little spurts of sound.

He did not know how he looked then, but Haüy, recounting it later, told of this "elfin, this sad, little dark boy who sat and swayed and brushed away his tears with irritation."

"Come sit with me here," the musical voice said softly.

He arose without his cane and went to the sound of the music. He felt a bench, seated himself beside her as she moved over. She rippled the keys, guided his small hands across them, too.

"This is a good language for the blind, think you not?" she asked. Her French was guttural and different.

"You are not French, madame?" he asked politely.

"No, I am Austrian," she said. "My name is Therese von Paradis. Do you know of it?"

"I confess I do not, madame," the small boy said.

"You are not very gallant, Monsieur Braille," Haüy said. "Madame is the most famous pianist in all Europe. She has played for crowned heads. She is the most popular concert pianist in Paris and in the capitals of Europe."

Braille said: "It is only because I am blind and ignorant that I have not heard of madame. You must excuse me," he said turning his blind eyes to her.

She caught him to her. "You are a diplomat and you are charming. You are old beyond your years. Monsieur Haüy has not exaggerated. You are very sensitive and accomplished. Let us see. What is it you wish? But let me tell you first. Let me help you find the richness in living I have found. Are you willing to study hard?"

"But very much, madame," he said. "Very much."

"You are lonely, too, in your blindness?" she asked wisely.

"Very lonely, madame. Very lonely. But not so much since I have come to Monsieur Haüy's school," he said.

"Ah, the diplomat again," she said. "We shall make arrangements. I have for long been sure that the blind can be musically accomplished more easily than the seeing. We shall see. Are you willing to let me experiment?" she asked. "It would be a great favor for me."

"*Oui,* madame," the boy said.

The great lady kissed him, pressed upon him not only the sweet comfits but the enameled box as well.

"A small souvenir," she said. "Do not forget me. Do not forget your blind brothers."

That was his first and last meeting with the fabled Madame von Paradis.

Therese von Paradis was born of rich parents in Vienna, and, like Braille, was blinded when very young. Her father, a man of vast perception, had early encouraged the girl to continue her musical career for which she had shown great promise.

At the age of fourteen, she had made her bow at her first concert in Vienna and had left the audience spellbound with the whimsicality of her technique. Later, she improved her style and became a master. She studied in the only manner she could. Her father hired a famous pianist to play for her by the hour and she picked up, painfully and painstakingly, both the notes and technique to the point where she surpassed her own masters.

During the next two years, except for a mad interval, Louis's life was enchanted. Daily, after his class work at the Institute, he was taken to the church near by and instructed on the organ. This instrument was chosen for him by Madame von Paradis as being the one that would best lend itself to the affliction.

She wrote to him just once, and he never heard from her

again, for she died soon thereafter in 1821. But he always treasured her letter.

"My dear Brother," she wrote him. "I have determined that the organ, which is the best instrumentality for holy music, should be your *métier*.

"The ears of the blind are closer to God than the ears of the seeing. The legs of the blind, which are forever stumbling and halting, are surer on the pedals than the seeing. I feel very sure that you will evoke from the organ strains which should be pleasing to the ears of those cast in semblance of God.

"Be sure that humanity will be more critical than God, however. Work hard. Do not try to be happy. That is impossible. But try to find contentment in the strains you lift up to Him. I shall be eager to hear from you and your progress."

Madame von Paradis later paid over to the organist at the church near the school enough monies to defray the cost of a year's tuition. Louis was to become one of the greatest organists and violoncellists in Europe.

IV A Window Rises

THE ORGANIST AT ST. ANNE'S CHURCH WAS GREATLY
perplexed when Haüy, leading the anemic-looking lad up
to the organ, placed his hand on the boy's head and said:
"This will be your new pupil, if you will take him."

He then told Raoul Delacorte, the organist, what Madame
von Paradis had offered and what she had suggested. And
he told him something of Louis's life and blindness.

Delacorte lifted his hands helplessly. "This is very un-
orthodox. How can I teach a blind one who has been blinded
since infancy? How will he read notes and understand the
theory of notes? If he had studied even a bit before he became blind, then there might have been a way. Frankly, I
should like to earn the extra money, and though I have a

great pity for the boy, I do not see how I can help him.

"Besides," he said, "what is the purpose? Of what use will it be to him even if I do succeed in teaching him?"

"Just to give him a fuller life, my friend," Haüy responded. "Moreover, you will find that he, like all blind persons, has a very receptive ear, a very acute ear and it may not be as difficult as you think. Just a little patience," and here he leaned forward so that Louis should not hear, "and a little gentleness."

Delacorte nodded, placed his hand on Louis's head, and asked, "Shall I play for you?" The boy nodded, sat down with Haüy on a bench. Soon there came a thin strain, then a swelling note, and the church was filled with music.

Delacorte played for a few minutes, ceased, and said, "That was the master Bach. If you play some day, you will play him very often, though he is not liked by many of the people in the musical world who do not like revolutionaries. But you will know more about that later. Did you know that the organ is one of the most difficult of all the instruments?"

"Madame von Paradis has told me," Louis said humbly. "But she also said it is one of the most satisfying."

The organist was greatly pleased. He clapped Louis on his shoulder. "You are a diplomat. We will make a musician of you, too."

Louis was relieved of some of his duties at the school and reported twice a day for a month at the church. That was the arrangement. If Delacorte found it impossible after a month, then the whole idea would be dropped.

Organs, at the time, were highly developed and highly complex though not so difficult as today. Louis would sit next to the organist on the great bench and as Delacorte would strike a note, he would listen with all his senses while his finger was held on the key. Then he would strike the note himself and listen even more raptly as the gigantic instrument gave forth with sound.

"You see how wonderful this is," Delacorte said, striking a key and setting up a tremendous sound. "There is a feeling of power here and if you can control this power, well then, you are an organist."

Then he explained the theory of the organ. How air rushes into pipes of various lengths as keys are struck and how the air sets up vibrations depending on the length of the pipe.

The boy listened, understood why the tremendous sounds and the tiny fluting sounds were able to be made with the striking of a key. Delacorte would play a few chords after Louis had understood a section of the keyboard and then tell Louis to play them back by ear.

The boy's perception amazed the organist and though he withheld comment until the trial period of a month was over, Louis could tell he was pleased when one day Delacorte told him that he had placed blocks of wood over the pedals.

"That's so your legs can reach them. You are too small for this instrument, you know."

That day, he tapped back to the school with melodies and chords bursting through his head. In his room, he waved his hands about and fancied he heard the great strains burst forth.

The month was soon over and Louis, in his raptness at learning something new, had indeed forgotten to mark the passage of the period. One day, he came in as usual and the organist led him up the two steps to the platform and said, "We will yet make a good musician of you. You have the feeling for it and it is easier to teach you than all of my seeing pupils. They see, my son; they have no vision. That is what you have," he added simply.

At the end of the lesson he told Louis to tell Haüy that he was very well pleased and that he would continue the lessons. "Not for the money, either, my young friend. Please tell Monsieur Haüy that I expect him to come here some day and hear you at your exercises. Now let us go to work."

Another month went by and Louis's existence began to take on a life apart from the school as music entered into him. One day, he shyly begged Haüy to accompany him and the good man did.

While Delacorte sat with Haüy on the bench near the organ, Louis gave his first concert. It consisted merely of a simple exercise but both men were enchanted with his flawless and unerring execution. They thumped him on his back and took him for a good dinner at a local café. While the men talked the politics of the day, Louis fell into the daydreams of a normal boy his age. "Some day," he thought to himself, "I shall earn my living from the organ and I shall play for the great of the world. This is the way out for a blind person, through the organ of hearing."

His friends at the school were mostly envious. Jean, and another boy, Josef, the son of a silk manufacturer of Lyons, were his only confidants. "You must learn too," he urged them enthusiastically. "You will feel different about yourself and the world around you. It gives you a feeling of power and freedom I cannot express. The good Monsieur Delacorte will help and I can help too, perhaps, after a few months when I know more. Will you come with me?"

Josef, who was sixteen and very large and very healthy for his age, guffawed. "My father would be pleased indeed if I were to tell him that I played the organ and that I wanted a career. He expects me to spend the rest of my life eating his food until he can marry me off to someone. Then he says he'll have to feed her too and our children as well."

Josef had lost his vision two years previously when he was stricken with a disease about which the doctors knew nothing. His father, who had many business contacts in Paris, had heard of the Institute and had enrolled him to "get me out of the way," Josef said.

Whether this were true or not, Louis had no way of judging, but he tried to explain that studying music was not for the purpose of earning money. "It just makes you feel good," he said limply. Josef scoffed again.

The other boys at the school were openly hostile. When he came in from the church, perhaps humming a bar or so, they broke forth into laughter. "Here comes the concert-master. Listen to his cane, too. Even that is tapping music," they said.

One day, as Louis was mounting the steps to his room, his cane was pulled out from under him by one of the boys and he fell sprawling to the bottom. He felt a sharp pain in his back and could not rise for a moment. A jeering voice in his ear, that of the school's bully, Ernest Montelard, told him: "You stop putting on airs. You'll be begging on the streets just as we will." Then Louis felt a sharp kick in his ribs and a shout went up all about him. The others had apparently been waiting for him to come in and had planned the attack.

He was about to get on his feet, humiliated and tearful, when he heard a great roar. It was Josef. Then he heard Ernest, begging for mercy and great thumps on the floor.

"You'll pick on a little one, will you? Then have this, and that, and that, you cow," he heard Josef say. Ernest burst into tears and thumped his way to the end of the room, crying for Haüy.

Haüy came running and he was angrier than Louis had ever imagined he could be. "What is all this? Isn't it enough that the world beats you? Must you beat each other? This is disgraceful."

He seized poor Josef and slapped him and Louis could hear Josef protesting. Then Haüy helped Louis to his feet and demanded to know what the fracas was about.

Louis said, "Monsieur, apparently the students here are envious that I am taking music lessons. That is all. Josef tried to defend me." He said nothing about Ernest. Haüy dispersed the students to their chores and Louis was put to bed for three days with bruises and sores. For the first time in his young life, there crept upon him a hatred and bitterness. He developed a loathing for the tapping of the canes all about him. He snapped at the servants who brought him food. Foul words, such as he had heard farmers use when they shouted at their horses and cattle, came to his lips.

Mostly though, he daydreamed of revenge on Ernest. "That nothing, that brute," he thought. "I will fix that animal."

When Haüy came to see him, he was insolent. "I have nothing to say to you, monsieur. You house a bunch of cattle here. I am not part of them. I do not belong here. After all, you must remember, I am a musician. I am not just another cripple, you know."

Haüy, tactful, kindly Haüy, was not alarmed. Nor was he offended. "All right, my boy. If you think you are too good for this place, then you may go. The boys meant no harm. They are cruel as all young boys are. Perhaps crueler because they are blind. But they meant no harm. Think on that." And he went away.

But Louis nursed his hatred and to restore his ego, he planned the most dreadful death for Ernest. "I will trip him and then I will do this and that to him."

That evening, he felt his way down the corridor and quietly opened the door to Ernest's little room.

He heard his enemy snoring, padded on bare feet to the bed, and then, seized by a fury that astonished him, he smote with his cane, and then smote again.

There was a great outcry and Ernest leaped out of bed bewildered and shouting with terror. Louis lunged in the direction of his voice and swung his cane again. He felt a dreadful impact and a horrible sound and then there was silence. But just for a moment.

Without knowing it, he himself had been screaming and yelling oaths. He could no longer find his enemy and in a fury, he swept his cane about the room, smashing at everything within his reach. There came a running of feet and other students burst into the room questioning and shouting. Then there was Haüy, and Haüy was holding him by the scruff of his neck and shaking him without mercy.

"Little murderer," Haüy shouted. "This from you? Take this," and he turned Louis over his knee and gave him a sound spanking.

The humiliation was more than the boy could bear. Followed by jeering schoolmates, he went to his room and remained awake most of the night, alternating between more vows of revenge and tears.

At dawn, he made a sudden resolve, flung on his clothes quietly, counted his small store of money hastily, and tiptoed down the steps to the door. He opened it and the cool, fresh morning breeze of Paris swept over him. He felt refreshed and emboldened. He stepped into the street and not until he reached the curve of the corner did he take up his tapping. He did not know where he was going but he didn't care so long as he could get away from Haüy, whom he now hated for humiliating him, and the boys, whom he called "barbarians."

Haüy's spanking enraged him more than any other thing. He had fancied that he had a special place in the master's heart, and here he had been treated just like anyone else.

He walked into an early *bistro* for a small wine and a *croissant,* one of those famous Parisian half-moon rolls. He went out and was soon attracted by the sound of great wagons rumbling across the cobblestones and the stomping of what seemed giant horses.

It was the market place where the farmers who lived on the outskirts of the city brought their produce and barnyard animals to sell. He heard the cackling of geese and the quawking of chickens, and once the squeal of a pig being unloaded from a big dray. His homesickness, both because of his chastisement and the sounds of the country, knew no bounds. He felt his way to a wall, sank down and began to cry. He was, after all, still a very small boy, very pale, and very thin, and very far from his parents.

He felt a stunning blow on his head, and dazedly turned his blind eyes upward, his crying hushed for a moment. "Get away from here, you little beggar. I've got to put my stalls up." He felt a sharp kick in his ribs and the pain almost made him faint. He got to his feet and hobbled away followed by the cries of the shopkeeper. "You beggars get out early, don't you? You put on a crying act because you think that way I'll give you vegetables for nothing. Here, have a vegetable for nothing!" And he felt something sticky and squashy smash him full on the back of his neck. It was probably a rotten apple.

A kind word might have made him cry more. But this was too much. He turned, wiping his neck with his kerchief, and said: "I am no beggar, monsieur, and I want nothing from you. Why do you strike and kick me?"

The man was taken aback. "Why, you little thief, how dare you answer me? All you blind are thieves and beggars and rascals. Take care, or I'll hit you again."

"Monsieur, I am no thief and no beggar, I insist. Would you give me a job?" It came to him that if he had not made a friend, he had at least made an acquaintance. After all, he knew no one in Paris to whom he could turn. The thought of going home to his parents, though he was homesick, was abhorrent. What was there for him there?

"Give you a job?" the man roared. "So that you can steal from me?" Then struck by cupidity, the man thought for a moment, and said, "All right, I'll give you a job, one meal a day and a place to sleep. How is that? But take care, I warn you. I will be watching you."

"What can I do, monsieur?" he asked with quiet dignity.

"Each day, you will sort the rotten vegetables from the good ones and put them in two piles. At night, you can sleep in the shop on a good bed made of sacks. If you're a good worker, I'll give you two meals a day. We shall see. No one can say Anatole Bouchard does not have a kind heart. You are young and so perhaps you have not become a great thief yet." And here, the man roared with laughter. It was a laugh that Louis learned to hate in the months that followed.

His work was not arduous except for certain times during the day when Bouchard made him drag great sacks from one end of the small shop to the other and pile them up. His heavy labors came at the end of the long day, which began at dawn, when he helped dismantle the stalls and pull the fruit and vegetables into the shop. Then, Bouchard pushed him into the small place, and without so much as a "good night," swung to a heavy iron door, put on a hasp, and locked him in with a gigantic iron lock.

He heard Bouchard's footsteps going away and he lay down on a pile of sacks smelling of the fields and fruits and vegetables. Soon, when there was silence, and darkness fell, out came the great rats, and gnawed at the potatoes, which they appeared to relish most.

The first few nights, Louis was awakened by Bouchard, who came to see whether his helper was robbing him. The

great hasp was lifted from the door and Bouchard said grum-
blingly, "Are you there?" Then he went away and Louis was
left to his thoughts.

He grew very filthy. He never washed or combed his hair.
Once, the wife of the fruiterer came into the shop with a
cumbersome pair of shears and said, "You look like a savage
from Africa. You are frightening away the customers, my
husband says."

He allowed her to cut his hair. Following that, she brought
him a basin of water and told him to wash himself that
night. "You smell very rich, my young friend," she said.

In an age when people didn't bathe frequently, Louis had,
however, come from a farm area where the people did swim
occasionally in near-by ponds and lakes. He did know that
he smelled very badly but he did not care. Each day went by
like the one before. He heard talk such as he had never heard
in his life, the coarse gutter talk of the slum housewives who
came to shop. Now and then, a gamin from the streets
snatched at his cane as he sat in the doorway of the shop,
and he learned to swing with it and swear like the best of
them.

Now and then he thought of Haüy or his parents and,
wallowing in self pity, it gave him great pleasure to think
that they were searching frantically for him. Other times, he
was sure that everyone was glad he was gone.

Despite the promise made by Bouchard, he never received
more than the one meal a day. That usually consisted of a

piece of bread and a thick soup made by Mrs. Bouchard. However, he was allowed to eat as much of the spoiled fruit and vegetables as he wished. Those were always in the last stages of decay when even the thriftiest Paris housewife would not buy them. But they were nourishing and though he slept like a pig in a sty and ate his scanty once-a-day meal, he gained weight and he could feel a new strength coming into his body. Ever introspective because of his blindness, he began to enjoy talking to himself as his adolescence grew upon him. He had feverish dreams that made no sense. He began to feel restless and his thoughts wandered into areas that frightenend him. He began to think of girls. But his past life, at home, at the school, at the organ, appeared remote, as in a dream.

"You are getting fat, you rascal," Bouchard said to him one day, and then gave out with that terrible roaring laughter.

"Not from your one meal a day, monsieur," Louis said insolently. His accent had taken on a new note; he slurred his speech as the poverty-stricken classes did.

He received a buffet in the head that sent him sprawling and he bounded back, his cane swinging to the attack. He felt it strike Bouchard in the face, and with his heart beating rapidly, he fled out of the shop into the street, and not caring where he went, ran into a wall, hurt his head very badly and sank down and waited for death.

He heard footsteps, but they were not the familiar ones of Bouchard. He heard no one coming after him. Passers-by just walked by him without stopping. A foul-smelling dog came and sniffed him and he swung with his cane again and sent the beast yelping away.

After a while, he got to his feet. Blood was congealing on his head. He stopped the next man and asked his way to the school. He felt humble, defeated, and yet proud in a way he could not understand.

It seemed a very long time since he had gone away. He felt his way to the familiar step to which he had been led by another stranger, opened the door and walked in. The old odors swept over him: the smell of the soup, the sour smell of unwashed clothing, the feel of the wooden floor with one of the slats that had come loose, and there was a silence. Then there was Haüy's voice, and Haüy's arms were about him, and Haüy was kissing him, and his tears started.

Then Haüy said: "You are very filthy. Your parents have almost gone insane hunting for you. We had given you up for dead. You smell just like the worst thing I have ever seen." And then came question upon question piling on him. And there was Jean holding his arm, and even Ernest, his great enemy, and his tears grew into sobs. He felt very good to be back after an absence of four months.

Haüy was very tactful the next day, after Louis had washed himself thoroughly. He sent a messenger posthaste to Coupvray and Big Louis came galloping up two days later. Louis's great adventure was over.

"May I continue my music?" Louis asked after he was

scolded by Big Louis. He could, he was told, but he must behave himself. He was put on probation at the school and Haüy promised that no one would scoff or jeer at him.

"Matter of fact, I count on you to help the other boys," he said. "Maybe you can get them interested in music, too."

V "The Eye Is Upon Me."

LOUIS WAS NOW FOURTEEN. HIS FRAME HAD AGAIN thinned. With the turbulence of his adolescence, his appetite waned; he worked hard at school and even harder at the organ. The organist was very pleased with him and allowed him free rein whenever the instrument was available.

Each day, he tapped his way to St. Anne's Church at four o'clock, two hours before evening Mass. He had those blessed two hours when he could control the mighty instrument in the great empty church. By ear, his feet moving steadily and surely, and his hands like a caress, he coaxed sounds out of the giant pipes that the master said were his envy.

"I can teach you nothing more," he said. Louis's feet now reached the pedals and he was using the wooden blocks for a pupil of his own. He enjoyed teaching and guiding the hands of his young blind pupil. It was good for his ego and it helped him catch his own mistakes.

At times the canon, who became a great friend later on, seated himself quietly in the rear and watched the gaunt boy handle the stops and keys and murmured to himself: "Just like a holy painting or like a scene on the stained glass window."

Louis received a great blow when Haüy died suddenly of a heart attack. A new master took over, but he was a pedagogue who did not believe that the blind should be taught anything cultural, but rather that they should learn useful trades.

Because of the great wars that raged across Europe, factories for the manufacture of cannons and bullets and guns were going full blast. The new master, Jacques Genet, believed that the blind, with their dexterous fingers, could do very well in these plants. He obtained a contract from the government to operate a small shop where bullets were made, and harnessed the pupils five hours a day at the process. Louis balked but had to work along with the others.

When he went to plead with Genet for more time at the organ, Genet told him: "You are talented at the organ, I know, but you are no better than anyone here." Then he said, "You may go now and never disturb me until I ask for you."

Louis felt Haüy's death keenly and composed, even at that

early age, a kind of requiem for him, called "Night Has Come."

It was a year of further tragedies for him. One day his only good friend, Jean, disappeared from the school and when Louis asked about him, he was told that Jean had been taken home to his illustrious family. Later, word came that he had died of tuberculosis.

Then, one day, a courier came galloping up to the school with a message from Mrs. Braille. Big Louis had died in his shop of a stroke.

He was sent on the post chaise to attend the funeral. He remembered his months in the vegetable shop where he was uncaring of his parents' desperation. He felt his eyes fill with tears. He heard his mother weep softly. He stayed with her for two months, slept, ate her good cooking. A man was hired to run the saddle-making shop, and now and then, Louis would go and sit in the old accustomed spot and smell the leather and dream while the stranger worked.

He was restless and he begged his mother to let him go back to Paris. "I have nothing to do here. Please come with me to Paris. We can live nicely there. I can continue with my organ. You can make friends. Please come with me. Life is very exciting there."

Mrs. Braille, in turn, begged him to stay. "I have no one now but you. Please stay here. We have enough money to live on for many years, though your father is gone. And we have a good income even though that pig of a hired man wants more and more every month. Please stay," she begged.

He missed his organ, the sounds of the robust Paris he had come to love. There was an impasse, and he asked his mother whether he might go back to the school for three or four months.

"If I am unhappy or if you want me to come back after that, I will," he promised, so she let him go.

A month went by and with that another begging letter from his mother accompanied by a whole box of baked goodies; a meat pasty that had spoiled somewhat en route, but which Louis shared and enjoyed with his friends. Before he could answer and tell her that he was too happy with music to come back to the empty life in Coupvray, another courier came to tell him that his mother was dead. She had survived her husband by only a few months. What she died of is now known as cancer. Then, it was known as the "wasting disease."

She left all her money to Louis and, for a blind teen-ager, he was very rich, but he was very sad and unhappy. The four persons dearest to him—his parents, Haüy, and Jean—had died within a short time of each other. When he needed them most, they were gone. His young crisis was acute. It was only at his organ that he was able to find peace. All about him, he could hear the sounds of the great city, spreading out, becoming aware of its functions as the "City of Light in the Western World," listening to the tramp of soldiers as they marched through the streets. He could hear the thin voice of

the drummer-boy keeping time to his beat, and he said to himself, "I would have been that . . . a drummer-boy with Napoleon's army."

He felt himself outside of life. His blindness cut him off
from the fulfillment of puberty; from young girls whose
voices he heard whenever he went out on the streets.

"What am I? What shall I do?" he asked himself. He felt
longings that were vague and formless. At his age, when he
needed emotional outlets so badly, there was no one to whom
he could turn.

On Sundays, he rented a coach and took himself to the
banks of the Seine where he sat under a tree and tried to
overhear what picnickers were saying. He rarely took food
with him, and he returned in the evening exhausted with
asking his way, with being led by strangers, and more lone-
some than ever.

He sought pity and attention and there crept into his head
a plan to find it. He left the school one Sunday, walked aim-
lessly to a crowded boulevard where the fashionable of Paris
paraded, and threw himself in the dust. "Why not?" he
thought defiantly. "Suppose my parents didn't have any
means and left me penniless? I would be a beggar,
wouldn't I?"

He held out his hat and moaned whenever he heard footsteps draw near him. He heard the clink of coins dropping
into his hat.

"That there is a well-dressed beggar, no?" he heard a

passer-by say. And he felt himself prodded with a foot. Then he heard a woman's merry laugh. "This is a fashionable boulevard and the beggars here must dress well, too," she said. They both laughed again.

He didn't mind and begging gave him a sense of excitement. It gave him the emotional attention he craved. At least he was not completely outside the busy life about him. And the woman's voice, though she was laughing at him, thrilled him greatly. He treasured the memory of her laugh for many weeks until it became transformed into a note of tenderness for him and not one of indifference and mockery.

Another day, he threw his cane away deliberately and said to himself, "Fine. This is splendid. I will find death this way. Here I am without a cane. I will go no place in particular. If I am run down by a horse, so much the worse for me. But they will be sorry."

He placed his hands determinedly in his pockets and tried to stroll on. He walked a few paces but his legs were stiff, they quivered with fright, and he could not go on. He began to totter, to weave on the street and then he halted, paralyzed.

He heard a voice in his ear. "You have lost your stick, my poor one." It was a woman's voice. He did not break down until he had gotten himself into the carriage which he asked her to hail for him.

In the carriage, he wept like a child. In his room, he asked himself: "Am I always to be a pathetic?" Yes, he told himself, he was always to be a pathetic.

He tried to keep a diary to put down his innermost thoughts. It was just another form of introspection, a popular hobby for an adolescent with a secret life. But his was more secret than most. He could not write of course, only print. He measured with his thumb to see how much space to allow for a succeeding line and then continued there with his pen.

Often he thought of Madame von Paradis and in his imagination she began to assume the face of his mother. The lines about his mouth grew more deeply etched; he looked thirty at the age of fifteen.

Then, at this crucial moment in his life, he found a place in the world.

The organist at the local Church of St. Anne moved from Paris and the canon, to everyone's astonishment, including his own, asked Louis Braille to take over. The canon, Richard Benoît, was in his own way a remarkable man. He had held a high post at the Cathedral of Notre Dame and through the exigencies of church politics, when he had dared to defy the bishop on a matter of theological hairsplitting, had been demoted and sent to humble St. Anne's.

He was thus a worldly man and had connections with persons highly placed in cultural circles. He was destined to affect Braille's life profoundly.

The parishioners of the district were amazed to see the young blind boy mount the rostrum of the organ. While he did not become an accomplished organist for many years, he had taken to the instrument very easily and it was at the organ, both mornings and evenings, that he was able to find surcease from his youthful torments.

He became very religious and wondered whether he should not find a place among the blind order of friars and shut himself away from the world.

"Wouldn't that be best for me?" he asked the canon with a strange maturity. "I have no friends, no mother, no father, no responsibilities except myself. What will become of me otherwise? Shall I beg on the streets later on? I tried it once," he admitted shamefacedly, "and I'd rather die."

"Be grateful to God for what you have now," the canon said. "Others in your position would be apprenticed out to strolling mummers. Or they would have some menial work at the almshouse. You are wrong for despairing," he said quietly. "Why do you need to worry about what will happen to you later on? You have wit, an eagerness to learn, a good musical bent, some money from your parents. As for friends, well, I do not have many either. I will be your friend. You will be mine."

He arranged for Louis to obtain an increased stipend for his organ work. Louis's wants were few and his appetite was very bad. His pitiful, wasted body, ravaged by a cough, seemed to shrink more and more. He dressed neatly, however, and spent a great deal of his funds on busts of composers. He fingered them with delight, ran his hands over their faces and dreamed that he, too, one day, would have a bust of himself for posterity

Talks with the canon took him out of himself a great deal. He heard tales about the great and the near-great of Paris and began to understand, after a while, that they too were human and had failings and deficiencies and blind spots.

He resolved to devote most of his earnings from the church to others, and subsidized the tuition of two students. This was evidence of how much the boy was the man, just how much older he was than his years.

The new director of the school, Professor Leopold Erhardt, a German, was more taken up with solitary bouts at liquor than with the welfare of his charges. Young Braille impressed himself on Herr Erhardt as a sensible boy and the director all but turned over the actual running of the school to Louis.

His life, at sixteen, thus became full. He ceased to mourn his lot and plunged into animated discussions with the canon and with Erhardt when the latter was sober enough.

He fulfilled himself at the organ and even ventured forth somewhat into the hectic night life of Paris.

This he was able to achieve through the strange interest of the daughter of the local baker from whom he had bought glacé cakes when he first had come to Paris. Denise developed a romantic attachment for him when she first saw him high above the worshippers, at the church organ. His pale face, surmounted by a fringe of curly hair, and his eyes looking upward, dramatically and beseechingly, at the stained-glass windows, captivated the young girl.

Whenever Louis came into the bakeshop, she talked with

him about his playing and she flattered him to the point where he was at times embarrassed. At other times, he thought to himself: "That's a very intelligent girl."

He thought of her often when he was playing and even more often in his room when he was alone. Her voice was fresh and girlish and it touched something inside him he couldn't understand. One day, tentatively, he asked her whether she would accompany him to the church sometime while he practiced. She agreed so instantly and so spontaneously that Louis was overwhelmed and he felt a great, warm happiness, a surge which he took to bed with him.

Another day, he called for her at the bakeshop, and talking as though it were nothing at all, though he had dressed very carefully in his Sunday best, he asked casually if she would like to go along with him. He was afraid she would say no, and he worried about what he would do under these circumstances. But again, she accepted with alacrity. He was astonished, but he wasn't aware of the talk she had had with her mother.

In those days, even the poorer classes maintained a close guard over young girls. Young girls simply had nothing to do with young men, never went on excursions with them, unless they were accompanied by a chaperone. The richer classes actually hired a chaperone, usually a widow of good standing. The lower classes, like shopkeepers, generally asked a relative to take over the function of safeguarding a young girl while she was with a suitor.

When Louis had first asked Denise whether she would accompany him to the church while he practiced, the young girl, obedient as most girls were in that day, told her mother about it.

"What do you think, *Maman?*" she asked.

The mother, tender and worldly-wise, thought for a moment. Then she said, "Those poor blind ones are harmless. I see no harm if you accompany him. Be discreet," she warned. "Do not develop a sentimental attachment for him. You are a healthy girl and a beautiful one. I think it is permissible to relax the conventions and you need no chaperone. After all, we are familiar with the blind students at the school and so it is somewhat different than if a stranger were to ask you to go somewhere with him."

"Yes," she said as an afterthought, for she was a generous woman, "yes, I think it would be a kind thing to do. And after all, he truly would be harmless." So Denise had no hesitancy in accompanying Louis.

As he tapped by her side, she put her arm through his, and said, "I will guide you." He could have knelt at her feet and kissed them, so great was his emotion. But like a man of the world, he said only, "Thank you very much. I know my way to the church." And to show his brave, foolish, silly independence, he disengaged his arm from hers and made small talk as he sauntered with her.

At the church, to his horror, he tripped on the steps and when she caught him, he was embarrassed again and humiliated. As they walked up the aisle to the nave, and as he mounted the steps to the organ, again he tripped and swore so lustily that she laughed and laughed at his embarrassment. He thought she was laughing at him until she said, "No. Louis—and I will call you that—no, Louis, I didn't think a saintly looking organist could swear that way. After all, I'm the daughter of a bakeshop owner and I hear the customers who come in."

Louis thrilled once again. This girl indeed did understand him and had great intelligence. He tried to play well for her as she sat next to him on the bench but he could not tell whether she was impressed.

He had planned the evening very carefully despite his casual air and when she said yes to his invitation to dinner, his elation knew no bounds.

He called a carriage, with her help, and they were soon off to an expensive, if crowded, place the canon had told him about. He spoke to her almost until dawn while she stared fascinated by the regally dressed women. At times, he could not tell whether she was listening, but he poured forth all his dreams about a reading system, all about his life in Coupvray, as he remembered it, the fact that he was practically running the school. He preened himself, he chatted, he made small talk, he stole some of the anecdotes that the canon had told him and used himself in them. The girl was over whelmed with the wine, the atmosphere, the thin, blind boy, the crowds, the good food and the way Louis spread his money and tips about. It was a startling evening for her and she fell more in love with him than he knew.

She confessed to a musical interest and Louis set about teaching her the rudiments of the strings. He bought her a violoncello and when her interest waned, taught himself by ear and was soon quite accomplished at that instrument. Soon he was taking Denise to concerts and plays and the pair were seen together at late night cafés and salons to which the canon had given him introductions. The girl was in a whirl and Louis was living almost a normal life—the life of a handsome and monied young man who was not blind. It was good for him and it fed his ego, his sensibilities and his dreams.

He took her grandly to a café noted for its political habitués, and he talked to her of women, of war, of peace, of Napoleon, of people—in short, of all the things with which he had never had contact.

"You are my eyes," he told Denise with dramatic intensity. She quivered and tears started in her eyes. It was a healthy life for him away from the narrow circle of the church organ and the school. He broadened out, affected mannerisms in speech, wore his hat at a new angle, and was very happy. After all, except for his eyes, he was normal.

From his café associations he made contacts with Parisian families who at first invited him to their homes out of pity, but later came to regard him as good company because of his wit and penetration.

Too, the youngster was humble within his affliction and flattered the egos of his new friends by asking their opinion on the stirring events that were sweeping the nation and the world.

"That is an intelligent one, there," friends would say, "though he is blind."

Out of these new friends, he made others and found a place for himself in the salons of the day where many from high places gathered. It was the fashion then in Paris for persons in political and intellectual circles to forgather at homes until far in the night, sipping coffee, munching fruit and testing their wits in friendly conversation.

At one of these gatherings, to which he took Denise, he was engaged in talk with an Alphonse Thibaud who asked Louis why "such as you do not attempt some way of reading and writing for the blind that might be better than the clumsy embossing method?"

"Look you," Thibaud said. "You are young, rich for a blind man, intelligent, and with all the time in the world. In this age of enlightenment, it might be a good chore for you to bend your efforts to the thing."

Braille spoke with a passion that astonished both the listener and himself. "What would you have us do, messire? It is easy for you to speak. What is it you mean?" he said bitterly.

Thibaud was taken aback. "I am sorry," he said. "I can

· 82 ·

well recognize how this must offend you. But it seems to me, with enough thought, some other method could be devised. I mean no offense," he said kindly. "Look. You know how little versed you are in life about you, how handicapped you are. Why is it not a good idea?"

"I will tell you why," Braille said. "It is the duty of the seeing to find some way. How can I, groping in the dark, do this? How easy it would be for the well to do this! I am not familiar with things that are commonplace to the seeing. How much easier it would be for the seeing!"

He went on. "You say I am rich. You say I am intelligent. No, I am nothing. My so-called riches were earned by a hardworking father, and my intelligence is a mockery. The Parisian street gamin knows more than I. No, I am nothing. It is for the seeing to help us. They can find the way," he said stubbornly.

"And what if the seeing don't care?" Thibaud said. "What if they don't care?"

Thibaud was voicing the great conflict that had come upon the world following the French Revolution—the question of whether one man was responsible for the well-being of his fellow, the new crisis in relationship that had come into play to shape the forces of the world and to mold history.

"There is a revolution in thinking today in the world," Thibaud said. "Perhaps it will reach across to the blind. It already has touched upon many areas, such as among the old and the very poor. What I mean is, perhaps a blind man can hasten what I admit should be the duty of the seeing to do, to help his blind brother."

Thibaud was a commercial counselor in the French government and thus very cautious in what he might say.

"Perhaps you have taught me something," Braille said, rising and reaching for his stick. "Perhaps, messire, you have taught me something. Come, Denise, I am tired."

Strolling through the narrow filthy streets of Paris, Braille was very thoughtful.

"What did you think of what that man said?" he asked her.

"I must confess I was greatly impressed," she answered. "I cannot see why it should be too difficult in this age of science," she added.

"You do not understand! Look, Denise," he said, stopping to face her. "Look at my eyes. I cannot see you. Can you not understand that? I cannot see you. I can see nothing . . ." his voice rose shrilly.

"See now," he said as though trying to press home an argument. "I will tell you: I cannot understand half the things you tell me that you read from a newspaper. I am away from life. Do you hear me?"

"What is this cannon you tell me about? What is the shape of a cannon? What do you mean when you tell me that British men have taken to new fashions? What is fashion? You tell me that you have a new pink bonnet. Splendid! In the name of God, what is pink? What is pink?" he shouted again.

Denise burst into tears. Louis was distressed. "I am sorry. I am sorry. Please do not cry. I have often spoken like this to myself. But, in the name of God—and I speak softly— what is pink? Please forgive me, what is pink?"

He wept in his torment and tore at his eyes on the street in the pale Paris moonlight while the girl wept and said over and over again, "Pink does not matter, it does not matter what pink is. Believe me, pink is not important." She kissed him lightly on his cheek and taking his arm, led him home, the while murmuring maternally to him.

It is from his diary that his anguish and despair at this point in his life may be gleaned. That morning, and for many another night, he wrote feverishly in his diary, that great, clumsy book so pitifully and painstakingly formed.

I will pose this question as scientifically as would a mathematician. I am blind. I cannot see. Is that clear? Splendid. So much then is clear. I am blind and I cannot see.

Now poses the question: How can I arrange to see? How is it possible for me to read that which has been set down by the seeing? About history? About art? About medicine? About politics? About women and men about me? About the mystery of birth and love? About Denise? What shall I do about her? What?

In short, how is it possible for me, a blind person,

to take my place in the world as part of the world?

How is it possible for me to take my place, not on a level with the seeing, for that is manifestly impossible, but nearly on the same level?

How is it possible for me to be able to read and write what is written not long after it is written, so that I am not too far behind the happening?

Is this then insoluble? It may be insoluble, but I cannot countenance that it be insoluble. I say here and now, if it is insoluble, then I shall destroy myself. I put this plainly to myself: If I cannot find a way to read and write and understand life about me, through some very classic, simple formula, then I shall kill myself.

How, now, come I by the word insoluble? This is a good word, so all is not hopeless if I know and use this word. All right, then. I came by this word through the embossing method. Before embossing, I would never have known the word, the big and important word, the educated word of "insoluble."

Before embossing, I would have been taught the "twig method." I would thus never have learned this beautiful word. I am thus very advanced. This is all very splendid.

Look, now, I can write. I can place my fingers across indentations on a paper and I can trace each letter by its shape and not by the way it looks. Splendid, again. I trace the words by letters alone.

The difficulty then resolves itself into the fact that I am trying to make my fingers fly as fast as can the eyes. Is this possible? No, this is not possible. It is, as a matter of fact, impossible.

Here he came to a dead stop in his reasoning.

Look, now, I came to learn how to read within the values of the seeing man. How conceited of the blind to try and use the same alphabet, the same formulas as the seeing use. How very ridiculous. Of course, that is ridiculous. Why should we confine ourselves to the things used by the seeing, when their way was developed for the eye!

We, we have no eyes. How terribly, terribly ridiculous it is for us to travel on paths laid out for the seeing. Why should the blind man, without eyes, think he can use the implements of the seeing? The absurdity is astounding. It is stupid, even.

There is something wrong in the entire setup. This is arrogance, this is insolence to demand that the seeing will wait for the blind to catch up, to think they will write slowly, will say things slowly, so that I can read them slowly.

The solution then rests with a device that has nothing to do with the eyes.

Shall it be in the ears? Our ears are as good as the ears of the seeing. They are as quick. Some say even quicker! Are sounds the answer? Can mechanical sounds be arranged? A kind of speaking with sounds? We shall see about this.

Is smell the answer? Our smell is also said to be sharper than that of the seeing. Shall some kind of incense slowly waft words to us by way of our noses? It is funny, but why not?

Is touching the best answer? The way we do it now? Is the sense of touch the finality? We shall see about that.

Just because we use the sense of touch now, does not mean it is the final answer. It is not good enough the way it stands now. Look how clumsily I write—how clumsily I read!

Perhaps it may be the sense of taste, the last remaining sense. Shall we taste words? This is funny, too, but not funnier than touching, for example. Why should taste, smell, and hearing be a funny way to read when touch is not? Why?

In his stiff, archaic, Norman French, in his laborious, aching, eking out of words in giant letters like some backwood schoolboy, he thus set down his dilemma, his crisis.

The letters of his diary are tormented, weave this way and that like the problems he posed. They are tall, and sharp-pointing, like his impatience.

He wandered to the window and stared out and he could

feel a stirring on his eyelids as light and shadow from the moon passed across them. He felt a slight twinge of pain as he ever did when light would strike across his eyes after he had sat in the shadows.

"Perhaps this is a miracle, this pain? Perhaps one of the canon's miracles he has told me of is coming true?" he prayed.

In his time, though it was not long ago as time is measured, men lived close to miracles and believed firmly in them.

A thought struck him. "Were I to recover my sight in a miracle, would I forget my blind brothers? Never, never, never," he vowed vehemently.

He thought to dare God. "Restore me my sight, try me, and see whether I will forget my brothers. Try me," he defied God.

But nothing happened. The pain passed and he fell into a deep slumber.

For the next few days he was restless. Then he asked for a month's leave.

"I want to go home to my village again. I must think and get away from here for a while," he begged. Leave was granted, and happily he packed and went off on the post chaise across the rough, winter-hardened road.

His leave-taking with Denise was very tender. She kissed him on his brow and gave him a little package of food for the road. The maternal touch stirred him. "You are like a sister to me," he said foolishly. Denise didn't like it a bit. And so they parted for a while, he with a sense of blown-up destiny and with an air of having "work to do," and she with a feeling of loss. Her mother scolded her severely and told her to forget that unresponsive man who thinks only of himself.

"You are a very silly girl. If he were rich at least, you might have a good marriage. But he is only a poor, blind man. We are richer than he is," she remonstrated with De nise. But the girl wouldn't forget or put Louis out of her mind.

VI The Horizon Nears

YOUNG LOUIS WENT BACK TO THE HOME OF HIS PARENTS. It was now occupied by a nephew of his father who had taken over the shop. He was kindly received, but he could not abide the smell of leather which pervaded the household. It reminded him of his misfortune and of the loss of his father.

He visited the old advocate, now very advanced in age. Louis and he talked of the village curé, now gone, and of petty village gossip.

"I would urge you to marry, my boy," the advocate, Georges Lamontoire, said. "There are plenty of young girls in this village who would gladly have you. You would be among your own people who know you, and know of your father and your father's father."

Louis shrugged with embarrassment. "No one would want me," he said. "Besides, I would not be able to know whether she is pretty," he added, permitting himself a rare levity.

The advocate waved a hand. "Suffice it that you are young and handsome yourself. You need someone close to you who would care for you." Louis again shrugged and smiled wanly.

"There are more important things," he said.

In his father's house, he had taken to his old room again, and there, with the familiar walls about him on which he could trace again the cracks in the plaster that had formed animals and landscapes for him through his finger ends, he was happy for a while.

But his melancholy, induced in part by the smell of leather, soon bore him down and he begged the advocate to let him stay with him and his family for a while.

"It is somewhat lonely for me in the old shop of my father, and you can tell me of the wonderful things you have seen and witnessed in your life in Paris?" he asked wistfully.

"You are welcome as my own son," the advocate said simply.

Lamontoire was not very much impressed in his subsequent talks with Louis about his determination to hunt a language for the blind.

"There are more important things," he said. "France is in turmoil. The world is in turmoil. The Church is scoffed at. A man today, if he has sensibility, devotes himself to larger affairs," he said airily.

"Besides, the blind are in great minority. You should bend your will to larger matters," he repeated. "Get married, have children, a home! In that, you will find much satisfaction. After all, there isn't much else even for a seeing person and in that way your life will be a more normal one."

Louis felt deflated as the advocate spoke. "You are young. You feel your handicap keenly. Perhaps more keenly than you should. I do not know why you should unless it be that you are a more sensitive person than it is given for the ordinary mortal to be. Many men have overcome afflictions without dwelling on them. I do not see why you cannot.

"Believe me, no one cares for the lame, the halt, and the blind.

"I am a materialist. I should like to urge you to invest your money—the money your father has left you—in something practical that will bring you an income, no matter how small. There are many farmlands hereabouts you can buy and have worked for you. Listen to me, my young friend. It is for this reason I am glad you came to Coupvray. I have been meaning to write you of this, anyhow."

Louis began to speak, and the advocate, seeing his chagrin, interrupted him. "That is not to mean you are wrong. It is all very worthy of you," he said, taking a sip of wine. "But do not feel you must concentrate solely on yourself and your blindness. Get out of yourself. You have some funds. Learn to live like other men young as yourself. There is a young widow not far from here to whom I have spoken of you. She would care for you well. Hers is a greater affliction. Her husband of a year was gored to death by a bull.

"Forgive me if I urge this upon you, but it would be well if you settle down, get married, get close to normal living. In your children, you will have comfort.

"You have suffered much," he continued. "What I am trying to say is, enjoy yourself." He turned to his wine with embarrassment.

Louis was silent for a long moment. He could almost see the young widow, smell a good dinner cooking and imagine himself with children. "Why not?" he asked himself. "Why not?"

Then he shuddered involuntarily. "Monsieur, I have the greatest respect for you, but you do not understand. You cannot understand. No one can understand." And his voice broke.

"It may be that I am too emotional because I am in Coupvray. I did not mean to break down," he said falteringly.

"We will talk of this later. Some other time. Let us eat now," the advocate said. And raising his voice, he shouted: "Ho, Maman, what have we for dinner?"

At the end of the winter, with the roads hard and frozen, Louis went forth one day on his customary walk. The snows had melted but an early, abiding spring frost had set in. The air was pure and clean. He lifted his head, breathed in, thought idly of what there might be for lunch and his mind strayed to the unknown widow. He brought himself back to thoughts of lunch. His appetite had never been so good. For the first time since he had come to maturity, he was living with a family, savoring the wholesome aspects of family life, and enjoying home cooking with a gusto. He more so, perhaps, for having been so long without a home.

As his cane tapped surely along the road, feeling for the soft tree mosses to keep himself on the pathway, he seemed to hear an echo.

He tapped, and an echo tapping returned. The clicking grew closer. Louis stopped but the clicking sounded again and he felt a presence near him with that antennae-like instinct which the blind themselves cannot explain.

"*Bon jour,*" he said pleasantly.

"*Bon jour,*" he heard a voice respond. "Was it you tapping?"

"It was indeed."

"Are you blind?"

"Are you blind?"

The questions came simultaneously. The two reached forward, found each other's hands, and shook.

"How generous are the households in these areas?" the blind stranger asked.

Louis was bewildered. "What do you mean—generous?"

"Come, come," the man said. "Can I get a meal around here? Can I get a bed to sleep in? I slept in a barn yesterday.

I have had nothing to eat since yesterday morning. The dogs chased me from the last village over that hill." He waved with his stick behind him.

"Come with me," Louis said with great distress. "Come with me. Have you no money?" he asked as an afterthought.

"You are a great jester," the blind stranger said. "You are moving me to hysterics. What do you mean 'do I have money!' Do they give you money hereabouts, the farmers?"

Louis did not answer but took him by the arm and led him sadly down the road to the village. In the warm room, where the great fireplace was crackling in the ancient chimney, Louis could hear the stranger shed his clothes. There seemed to be many of them. A smell of decay arose in the room that was almost suffocating.

Louis begged the advocate's wife to feed the man. When the food was served up, the man uttered sounds Louis had never heard from a human being. He seemed like some beast. Louis was sickened and ashamed.

From the kitchen where the blind beggar was growling and snapping over his food, Louis tapped his way to the parlor. "I am sorry. I am sorry. I did not know it would be so."

"What would you?" the advocate asked. "He is blind. He is a professional beggar. I am not being contemptuous. I am again being a realist. What else is there for the handicapped? I do not mind telling you, as you must know by now, that your parents were unusual. Count yourself lucky! I cannot help but tell you again had your parents followed the usual pattern, they would have sold you to some miserable farmer to work for him forever.

"I hope you count this as an object lesson. I urge you to invest your money in something that will keep you from a similar fate. I am a friend in so telling you!"

Louis tapped his way to his room upstairs, seized an armful of clothes, and tapped his way down with them. On the kitchen table, he emptied his pockets of money and placed all before the stranger.

"What is your name?" he asked him with embarrassment.

"Name? Name of name, what do I need a name for?" the stranger asked fiercely. "To tap the roads I need a name? What nonsense is this?" he demanded.

"How about some food for the road?" Louis asked.

A packet of food was prepared for the stranger and he was set upon the road. But not before he had whispered, with his foul breath, in Louis's ear: "You have a good little arrangement here, have you not, my friend?" Louis said nothing, but stood on the road until the stranger's tapping was lost to his sound.

"I do not know how fortunate I am, I suppose," he said to his host that night after a lengthy silence.

"No, Louis, you do not," the advocate said violently. He tapped vehemently on the hearthstone with his pipe. "I could not have hoped for a better example for you to witness. What you saw and what you heard is typical. You do not know how fortunate you are.

"Believe me, I am your friend. I am like a father. I remember when you were blinded and I have spoken numberless evenings with your parents about you. I commend you again to see the error of your ways. I ask you to leave that school and to settle down. You have enough money not to be forced to work. You can have a good farm, and employ others to work for you. You will have security. Listen to me, my boy, before it is too late!"

Louis nodded, said nothing. "I will not argue with you, my dear, good friend. But, there is so much you do not understand. My life is nothing . . ."

The advocate emptied his pipe, strode up the steps, each footfall a reproach.

That night Louis did not sleep much. Early the next morning he found his way to the little church where he had often gone with his parents. He sat in the rear pew of the cold church and listened to the silence.

"What am I doing here?" he questioned. "What am I doing here? I belong with the blind beggar. I am a traitor to him because of my comforts while he lives on the world like a dog, being snapped at, and snapping back."

"He is at least among his own kind occasionally, fulfilling his own destiny. I am a mockery of a human being, living in comfort. I have a guilt."

For a moment, he was tempted to walk out of the church, tap his way down the road and lose himself in the world as a beggar.

"What have I to lose? Food? Warmth? Clothes? Why not?" He felt himself ennobled with the thought and filled with high resolve. Then the stench of the beggar came back to him. "Is that ennobling? Is that high resolve? What will I prove through that?"

Then, musing along, he accused himself of cowardice. "I rationalize my comfort. I make myself feel better. I tell myself, within my blindness, that I am set apart. I am a great swindler. Why do I not walk out and join him down the road? I know why. I am a great swindler, that is why. I am frightened, that is why. I have contempt for myself for I am sheltered and soft."

His confusion grew greater and he wept softly for a while. After that, he went down the aisle to the little organ, seated himself, felt for the keys and pedals, and lifting his head, played softly.

He played until he was eased and until the thin noonday sun came through the ancient stained-glass windows.

Then he spoke aloud: "This, I vow. I will not ever forget my brothers." He felt the warmth of the sun more strongly on his face and his feet reached out more firmly on the pedals as contentment and surety stole upon him.

A few days later, he set out for Paris with a determination that was to be unflagging the rest of his life. He was never to swerve from his vow to improve the lot of the world's blind. Neither illness, nor scoffers, nor his music (the latter his chief and only pleasure), was ever to stay him. He was a man dedicated. The chance meeting with the blind beggar had resolved him for good.

The times were not ripe for experiment or for enlisting the aid of persons of wealth in an affair of social emotion, such as the lot of the blind man.

The Congress of Vienna had taken place following the downfall of Napoleon. And though the strongly worded decrees of the Congress of Vienna spoke much of the liberty of man and his well-being, they remained but words.

Too, a period of reaction had set in. The whole of Europe was dominated by men of conservative tastes who cared only to keep things just as they were. They were men whose interests were best served by maintaining what was called the status quo; they fought against change.

Many persons or agencies which might have abetted Braille in his dedication were taken up with their own misfortunes. Prices were then in collapse, taxes had risen, the farmer had no one to sell to and unemployment was rife. It was a poor time to get anyone to shed a tear over a blind man. At another time Braille might have been more fortunate and he would have had an easier course.

It is significant that many, many years were to pass before Braille was to have recognition for his reading and writing course. History never disappoints; it is never more nor less, but always fulfills the slightest movement. Braille was to be part of that tortuous and agonized and unrecognized movement. There was just too much disinterest for anything else.

But beneath the reaction, the distress, and the indifference, the period in which Braille strode mightily—he began his serious efforts at the age of seventeen in the year 1826—was a period of much thinking.

This thinking period was to evolve into a period of doing. Men, influenced by the French Revolution, began to question whether misfortune and poverty were ordered by God, as indeed those in power had claimed for centuries.

Scientists began to break away from the old shackles, one of which, for example, was the claim that childbirth must and should be accompanied by pain.

Men began to look to the stars and beneath the ground. This renaissance, this seeking and striving, was to materialize into the fantastic discoveries and inventions later on in the nineteenth century which paved the way for our own startling century.

Braille was one of the countless dreamers who, below the surface of conservative and ruling taste, continued to muse quietly of a better world.

He was no historical accident. The world was charged with such as he. There were some who dreamed of ships that would not be dependent upon the wind for their speed and direction. There were some who dreamed of vehicles that would travel through the air. There were many who dreamed of boats that would traverse the bottom of the sea.

Then, there were doctors who were impatient with the theory that such and such an illness meant certain death.

There were men working on better false teeth and other men, still, working strenuously to develop painkilling drugs.

In industry, at the time, there were men of vision who questioned whether mankind was destined to be a beast of burden and whether there were not ways of doing things more easily, whether there were not ways of harnessing the physical properties of nature to do man's bidding.

Among those thinkers, who upset the order of things in the wake of the French Revolution, there were men like Braille who did not count as human flotsam those handicapped by birth or accident.

Unknown to Braille all his life, there were men who were setting up statistics to prove that the majority of the blind became sightless not through accident but through disease. These men tried to show that congenital blindness could be prevented. These were the forerunners of what we know today as the pioneers of preventive medicine.

There were men working on artificial legs and arms for amputees, and there were still other men working on devices for the deaf and deafened.

Braille was not alone in his effort to find a doorway for the blind. Across the seas in America, also unknown to him, there were other men incited with the same devotion and dedication.

Had Louis known of this, he would have been greatly heartened. His life, except for his music, would not have taken on the loneliness and grimness that seem to afflict the giants of civilization in the course of their efforts. Braille, like other men of genius, felt he was alone, a voice in the wilderness.

International societies had not as yet developed to the point where there was an interchange of ideas from one country to another. Translations of research were very infrequent. There was a duplication of effort in every field of human longing that was heartbreaking through the nineteenth century. A man developed something and then learned to his astonishment that another man, in another country, and often in the same country, had come to the same conclusion, perhaps almost at the same time.

So beneath the currents of a very disorderly world, which was attempting to pick up the feudal pieces that had been left by the French Revolution, Braille and thousands like him dreamed and strove and broke their hearts.

We have never known giants like those nineteenth century giants who had no homes, no families, no kindred spirits to understand them. They understood nothing other than that they must strive, and as a rule they worked alone.

Many, like Braille, died at an early age, completely worn out. Many, like Braille, achieved what they set out to do. Many did not, and so are unknown to history. Braille, but for an accident, might also have been unknown to history.

VII The Flint Sparks

BRAILLE WAS NOW ENTERED UPON THE MOST IMPORTANT
phase of his life, the happiest, most rewarding, and the most
frustrated and bitter. For eight years, he had found peace in
his music, and he had become one of the greatest organists
and violoncellists in Europe.

From his musicianship he had gained much pleasure, personal fame, and more important to him, funds to carry on
his research into a system of reading and writing for the
blind.

In between, he continued to teach at the Institute. His
daily program exacted much from his health. Never robust,
his cough grew worse, But he didn't care and waved away

exhortations from those close to him to care for himself. He plunged deeply into his organ studies and speedily became a master to the point where he gave a concert in Paris at the age of twenty-five that was acclaimed by the greatest musicians in Europe. Too, he wrote many compositions with the aid of friends who guided his writings and his pathetic attempts to put on paper that which sang within him.

He ate little and continued to roam the streets of Paris, alone.

He was invited to many musical salons and usually went accompanied by Denise. After one of his recitals he delivered a talk on whether the blind had not been set apart to make music for the world.

"Acuteness, sense of color, and the sharp hearing sense is instinct in the blind," he argued. "We, who are deprived of color in nature, the greens and blues they tell me about, find a haunting remembrance of those colors within us.

"Why should not the governments of Europe set up great schools for the musical education of the blind? This is not a bad theory, my friends. Think of the thousands of blind persons who can take over a great section of our culture and give it new form and accomplishment. Why not?"

Paris, at the time, had more thousands of blind persons than at any time in its history. These were veterans of the Napoleonic Wars.

Emboldened by the applause with which his theory had

been greeted, one day he gathered more than a hundred of the blinded veterans at the hall of the Institute to test his theory.

"Messieurs," he said at the first address, "you have a chance to show the world that you are not set apart as a special class. Also, you have a chance to earn a living in a dignified manner. Please bear with me and try to study hard. In a year, in six months perhaps, many of you will be persons of worth and dignity—all through music."

Later on he confessed that he was merely trying to find a place for the blind in the world. "I could never get over the notion that we are chosen people and music seems like such a charming way to prove it."

He was looked upon as a madman for his mass-teaching experiment. His friends in the musical world sneered and declared that talent, and not blindness, was the requisite.

Be that as it may, Braille's theory was not proved or disproved. A handful of his blind veterans persisted and became fairly skilled at one or another of the instruments. But most of them, sad to say, were more concerned with finding a warm place to sit and a warm bowl of soup that went with each lesson than the theory itself.

The government at the time was forced to pay out a small bonus and pension to all handicapped veterans, so great were the number of professional beggars left over from the wars. And so, Braille's class soon dwindled into the very few who loved music and showed talent.

Braille defended himself and his theory by saying that his notion was not so much wrong as the fact that his blind classes were composed of "professional soldiers who had little interest in scholarly affairs as music."

That he was not completely wrong is evidenced today by the number of blind persons throughout the world who are accomplished singers, violinists and pianists.

In 1826, the exact season of the year is unknown, Braille was sitting in a café idly listening to the news of the day being read to him by Denise, his faithful companion.

He sipped wine, and listened to a long account on the thinking of a British philosopher, Jeremy Bentham, who emphasized the theory that governments had some responsibility for the well-being of citizens or subjects.

"This man is taking us out of the jungle," Braille commented. "Of what use is government, then, if not to concern itself with its citizens?"

Denise continued to read about Bentham's theory of a government based on "law and morality" where he attacked the so-called "natural" laws of economy.

"He is right, he is right. How do the 'natural' laws work out, for example, for my blind men?" Louis questioned. "Do they find a 'natural' place in the economy? Is it 'natural' for them to be beggars and thieves? I am sure it costs the economy more to put them in prison and chase them up the highways than it would if they were given productive work to do where they could support themselves."

Denise saw that he was getting aroused. Of late, Braille grew easily irritable. There was nothing sparking his life. He saw no future for himself. He had been feeling defeated and purposeless.

She turned to another story in the newspaper. Braille listened idly, then he leaned forward, and his face tightened. His sightless eyes shone and fixed on her.

"M. Charles Barbier, a former army captain," the account read, "wonders whether his system of night-writing could not be made available to the blind for development."

"Read that again. Read it again!" Braille shouted.

Denise read the article again. It said that Captain Charles Barbier, of the French Army, had invented a system whereby an outpost at the front could get a message from another outpost and read it without the necessity of striking a light.

In short, his system set up a series of code punches in thick paper which left a bulge. By tracing the finger along indentations created by the punches, such simple expressions as "enemy moving up on the left," or "open barrage attack," or "please send reinforcements," could be read in the darkness.

Men at outposts, the captain argued, could be easily trained to recognize these indentations. For example, he said, a circle raised like the cone atop a volcano, could mean: "We are encircled." Or a triangle could mean: "An attack is coming at three points," and so on.

These ridges could be made with a sharp awl that would

not quite pierce thick paper but push the other side up enough to form a permanent, staying ridge.

Braille sank back into his chair and meditatively sucked on his cane top. "This is embossing all over again," he murmured. "But it is embossing with a new twist and self-wielded."

A thought struck him. "In the name of God," he shouted. "In the name of God," he exclaimed again, thumping his cane. "This is it. This is it." Denise arose, frightened and embarrassed. "Louis, Louis, calm yourself," she said, glancing about the café.

"I tell you, Denise, this is it!" he shouted again, executing a kind of caper about the table, and seized the paper she was holding.

The café patrons stopped eating and talking and the room became still as the sightless man held the paper in front of his eyes as though by some superhuman will he could compel himself to see.

He continued to shout with excitement, and as the café proprietor came running, he fell back into his seat, tears streaming down his face.

The proprietor said kindly: "Monsieur Braille, I beg of you, calm yourself. You are disturbing my guests."

"You must forgive me, my friend," Braille said. "I am very happy. The task is now simple. But then, you do not know what I am talking about. Here," he said, flinging a handful of money on the table, "here, I buy a carafe of wine for each person in this room to celebrate. History has been made here."

Denise came to his side. "Louis, Louis, you are frightening me," she murmured. "Louis, please . . ."

He seized her and hugged her. "Aha," he said with emotion, "be not frightened, my poor child. Tomorrow, I will buy you a gown that will stun all Paris. You will turn a duchess green. You deserve it. I will tell you why later . . ."

She helped him from the table and kept edging him to the door. The patrons watched with the distress and embarrassment with which all blind persons are regarded.

"That one there is in a bad way," Louis heard one say.

"Not for long, not for long," he said cheerfully over his shoulder.

He could not contain himself with excitement as Denise led him to the Institute. "You must help me tomorrow," he urged. "We must find Captain Barbier."

That night he paced his room and thought until he felt his head would burst. He could not rest until he knew more. His brow was hot and he drank quarts of water throughout the night.

At seven o'clock in the morning, he presented himself at Denise's home, haggard and worn. His classes were taken over by a substitute.

"Louis, Louis, you are making yourself sick," Denise said softly.

Louis stroked her hair, and said, "Do not worry about me, my little one. I am very happy."

He went to St. Anne's with her to tell the canon he could not play that day.

"I go on God's work," he told him. The canon looked at Denise. She shrugged helplessly.

"Louis, what is the difficulty? Can I help you? You appear distraught," the canon said placing a hand on his shoulder.

"I must work this out myself," Louis said. He was almost dancing with impatience. "I see it all. Not clearly, mind you. But I see it," he kept exclaiming. "Come, Denise. Come, child."

They hailed a carriage and drove rapidly to the office of the newspaper in which the article had appeared.

No one was in attendance but a scrubwoman. "The office of the editor does not open until noon," she told Louis.

"This will never do," he said. "Where does the editor live?"

She told him, and away they sped to the home of the editor in a Paris suburb.

There Louis aroused the poor man from his bed and demanded to know where he could find Captain Barbier. The editor did not know what he was talking about.

"Monsieur, I see you are an afflicted one. Perhaps afflicted in more ways than one," he added acidly. "But does that necessitate arousing a good citizen from his uneasy slumbers and demanding to know things that make no sense? What do you want? Who are you?"

Braille tried to explain about the article.

The editor recollected immediately. "Ah, yes," he said. "You must go to the home of the writer of the article. Monsieur Prietre. Here is his address now and my best wishes."

Away they sped through the crowded streets back to the heart of Paris.

Denise led Louis up the steps of a rickety house. They climbed and climbed and there seemed to be no end to the climbing. On the very peak of the house, there was a little card in the door with the name of the writer on it.

Louis beat with his cane and beat again imperiously. A surly voice came through the door.

"Who is it?" Louis repeated. "Who is it then you wish to know, indeed? This is history rapping at your door, my friend. Get up and show your respects to it."

A head wrapped in a nightkerchief appeared. "Are you mad? What do you want?"

Louis told him briefly.

"That appears little reason to awaken a man in the middle of the night. It could have kept. Why it is not yet noon!"

"Frankly," the writer said, "I obtained my material from a technical article in the official military journal." Prietre gave Louis the name of the publication and away he sped with Denise to the Ministry of the Army where Prietre said the author was sure to be known.

There were difficulties at the ministry. Lists were consulted. Important people shunted Louis out of the way and took precedence over him. More lists were consulted by a puttering, mumbling old civil servant.

It was not until very late in the afternoon that the address was found. Through the day, neither Denise nor Louis had eaten. They sat humbly on a hard, uncomfortable bench in a draughty corridor.

Denise begged Louis to return home and rest and change his clothes before going out again. He now presented a bedraggled appearance. His cheekbones stood up high, and the stubble on his face gave him the appearance of a man close to death.

But even now he could not contain himself while they waited for a carriage to come along.

"Bear with me," he begged her. "I know you are tired but these drivers will cheat me and rob me and will thre me into the street. I pray you, bear with me. You know are like beasts with a blind man."

Denise pressed his arm. "But of course, Louis. I was merely thinking of you."

They proceeded to the home of Captain Barbier which was still at another end of Paris. Night had fallen when they reached the house. Luckily, Barbier was in.

Braille stood in the doorway, his head bowed deferentially. "Monsieur, I come to you on a matter of transcendental importance. I beg of you to give me some moments of your time."

The captain looked curiously at the disheveled man and the young girl holding protectively to his arm.

"Please come in. Pray seat yourself here," he said gently, leading him to a chair.

"Because of this high moment, what I have to say I prefer to say while standing," Louis answered with simple dignity. "Monsieur, I speak for myself. But also, I speak as well for all blind men living, and for those blind to come. Will you not tell me or give me instruction in your method of night-writing? I feel very surely I can adapt it to the needs of the blind as you suggested."

"But, of course," the captain said. "It is no military secret. I, myself, suggested that it be adapted."

"For that, too, I thank you most humbly, sir," Braille said. "It is rare today to find an interest in the blind on the part of the seeing. Very rare."

Barbier finally coaxed Braille into a seat, ordered wine and food, and then they spoke until midnight while Denise nodded in her chair.

"My poor Denise, my poor eyes," Braille said as they departed in the captain's own carriage. "You must be very angry with me and very tired and perhaps you will not wish to be my eyes any longer."

"I am not angry, Louis. I am very happy if you think you have chanced on a way. Perhaps if you do, you will have peace, and perhaps when you find peace," she added shyly, "you will think of other things." But Braille was not listening. He was too tired to hear anything but his own inner mind.

Using Barbier's method as a basis for operation, he spent the next three years, until 1829, in persistent, dogged and dedicated work.

His unremitting labors, which killed him at the age of forty-two, never ended until he developed the facile, elastic and perfect code. But many weary weeks and despairing months went by until he did.

VIII "I See the Dawn."

FOR TWO YEARS BRAILLE PUNCHED AND PUNCHED WITH a bodkin into miles of soft paper. He tried codes that embraced the signs of the zodiac. He tried codes that used mathematical symbols, as he had in his youth. He tried to discover whether aborigines in Australia, who were reputed to speak in short gutterals, spoke in a code he might adapt.

In his head there danced symbols and signs and letters and theories. Sometimes, he would be afflicted with shooting pains and at times his cough wracked him to the point where a seizure would bring him to his knees.

He never ate unless he was reminded to eat. His days took on a pattern reminiscent of all fabled seekers. His funds ran out and he gave concerts on the organ to replenish them.

All the while, he was teaching five to seven hours a day. He grew thinner and thinner, and with his emaciation, Denise's mother love for him grew.

After a year of effort and experimentation, he was able to develop a code that was perfect for someone who already knew how to read and write. It was then that he despaired greatest simply because the bridge of knowing how to read and write was first necessary.

"Then must come the unlearning and the teaching of my code," he said helplessly.

For every letter of the alphabet there were a limitless number of mathematical possibilities in the number of punches. For example, he arrived at a code where just two punches meant the letter "A" but then found that when he came to the letter "W" he would need about fifteen punches.

"This is no better than the embossing method," he said, destroying his beautifully conceived alphabet again, and starting anew. "This way, a blind man would have to carry a knapsack of paper with him in order to write a sentence," he said, laughing without mirth.

He enlisted the aid of military men who worked with codes. But they were of little use. They operated with what Braille termed "sweeping eyes," that is, they could take in whole lines of a code with a glance and then transcribe.

"They work with eyes. What have I to do with that? It is another world," he said.

Trial and error. Trial and error. The process continued endlessly. He even attempted musical symbols.

"Look," he said to his friends of the musical world, "look at the amazing array of sounds, embracing seven basic notes and five lines and spaces of the staff.

"With these, we use multifold variations to achieve all possible sounds known to the human ear. Let us see if we can boil these notes down and translate them into the reading and writing alphabet."

It was no good and all much too complex. He fell back on dots. And one day he got the notion of dots in variation, that is, of dots that could be interchangeable with what he called "the alphabet folding back upon itself."

Out of this, he finally came to his key, his famous "Braille cell," as it is called. The "cell" has not only withstood the test of time but created acrimonious debate throughout the world by persons concerned with education for the blind, and the blind themselves.

It was after refining his own system that he discovered to his amazement, while toying with the code, that he could do simple arithmetic with it, algebra, and higher mathematics. He also speedily discovered that he could use it for his music.

So perfect was his "cell" system, and he himself never was to know of its perfection, that it can be "translated" into every form of human endeavor and understanding.

To the uninitiated, the Braille system looks complex. But it is fairly simple after some close examination.

The cell itself is two dots wide and three dots high. It has the advantage of being more easily legible than the embossed Roman letter and may be written by hand with a simple device known as the Braille slate and stylus.

Braille's old theory that the blind must depart from the mechanics of the seeing in order to effect writing and reading was only too true.

The apparatus today, and it is not much different from the device used by Braille himself, consists of a board with a surface grooved horizontally and vertically by lines one-eighth of an inch apart.

Over this board, a frame is fitted like that of a common map delineator and one or more sheets of paper being placed over the board, the points are made with a bodkin through a slip of perforated tin, which contains all the variations used in the system.

The perforated tin has six holes in it, like this:

∙ ∙
∙ ∙
∙ ∙

As the sheets must be reversed to be read, the writing is from right to left, so that it can be read left to right. Several copies can be made at one time.

As Braille devised the code, there are forty-three symbols.

These include the entire alphabet, all the diphthongs, and the marks of punctuation. Ten fundamental signs form the basis of all the others.

These ten signs represent the first ten letters of the alphabet and the ten arabic numerals:

A	B	C	D	E	F	G	H	I	J
1	2	3	4	5	6	7	8	9	10

By placing one point under the left side of each fundamental sign, the second series is formed comprising the next ten letters. By placing two points under each fundamental sign, the third series, comprising U, V, X, Y, Z, C (C soft), E, A, E, U, is formed.

There are many other variations. As a matter of fact, using the ten basic signs, the variations are practically limitless.

Astonishingly, the system has been applied in such a manner as to make the reading and writing of music easier for the blind than for those who can see.

The Braille musical notation, with the various refinements developed by Braille's successors, is capable of expressing practically every musical character necessary for reproducing the most complicated composition.

Cautiously, cautiously, he experimented with his dots which he called "frozen taps." He toyed with them, made a few refinements after the first full burst of inspiration and hugged himself. "I find no fault here," he shouted after each test.

He practiced until he was sure, very sure. He then gave himself a week's vacation, slept, ate well, walked the streets happily. For the first time in his life, he felt warm and enriched.

"I have done it. I have done it," he said over and over.

One day he called Denise into his room, asked her to select any random bit of printed matter and told her to read slowly.

As she read in her clear, charming French he punched away through his tin perforator with the six holes.

When she had read perhaps ten paragraphs, he asked her to stop.

He reversed his paper and, feeling his way, smoothly read off, word for word, what she had read.

"Eh, what think you? Eh, my child? What do you think?" he demanded dancing about the room.

It was incredible to the girl. It was a miracle she could not fathom. "Louis, you will excite the whole world," she said.

With the surety that he had something to offer, and with great pride, he called for a meeting of the Institute staff and the senior pupils.

"Gentlemen, you may have heard of some mysterious goings-on these past few months. I am now ready to show the results. I offer these results in the name of the Institute and in honor of our founder, Haüy.

"Armand," he asked one of the servants, "please read any

selection from any volume or periodical you may find handy."

Louis seated himself with his little frame and his bodkin. As Armand read, he punched away busily with a curious, happy expression about his mouth.

The voice droned and Louis punched. Nothing could be heard but the voice and the slight tearing sound as the bodkin bit into the thick paper. The tearing sound was like a hiss, like the beginning of a new tongue.

After ten minutes or so of reading, when he could sense that the audience was getting restless, Louis called out: "Enough. I will now proceed to read back what has been read." And in a modulated tone, and with his voice breaking at times, utterly out of variance to the theme he was reading —it was a treatise on biology—Louis read what had been voiced.

Now and then he stumbled because of his nervousness. Now and then, a scientific word stumped him so that he was forced to retrace his fingers.

But the words came tumbling out almost as fast as Armand had read them.

When he came to the end, there was a silence. Then a great babel of voices broke. From the rear, there came a strident voice, that of the new director, Dr. La Porte, who had taken over from the sottish Erhardt.

"This is some trick. He has memorized it all. I have heard what is going on here in this school under my very nose. I say he has memorized it all."

There came a buzz of voices, expostulations.

Louis interrupted: "But, Dr. La Porte, I will be only too happy to repeat the experiment with any selection you yourself choose. I do not understand . . . You are mistaken," he shouted as La Porte tried to say something. "I have memorized nothing. I am amazed at this reaction." He and La Porte had been good friends; if not close, then certainly with a mutual respect. "You select the passage, and you select the reader," Braille said defiantly.

"Enough of this nonsense and let us go to our classes," he heard La Porte say brusquely. He heard chairs being pushed back and he was left alone on the little dais.

Except for a student who brushed by him and said, "Monsieur Braille, many students have great confidence in what you have done," he heard nothing from anyone.

That evening, he sought out La Porte in his study. "Why have you opposed my method?" he said straight out.

"It is a trick," La Porte said stubbornly. "And if it is not a trick, then it is foolish. We have a large investment here of books in the embossing method and your method would make our technique obsolete. Now is not the time for experiments. We have lost the support of many private benefactors. We cannot embark on anything new."

"But, Monsieur Le Directeur—" Braille said helplessly.

"As a matter of fact, I forbid you to hold any more demonstrations," the director said sternly.

Braille crept to his room, nonplused, bewildered.

He sought out the canon the next day at St. Anne's. "Why?" he questioned. "Why?"

The canon was a very seasoned man, one of those rare people who knew the world as well as things of the spirit. "It may be a simple case of jealousy," he said shrewdly. "Or perhaps M. La Porte is telling the truth. Perhaps this is not the time for experiments. There are experiments going on in many fields these days that are meeting with opposition from those who label progress 'revolution.' "

Again, he sought out the director and was this time sternly rebuked.

"Understand, Louis, I have nothing against new methods. But I will speak plainly. We have a school full of pupils. Many of them are having their tuition paid under the new government benevolence. To try and extend our curriculum would mean that we would come in for criticism.

"Too, we would have to unlearn everything we have taught our students. We would, in effect, be confessing to inadequacy, to being old-fashioned. At one blow, your method would shake the foundations of what we have built up. There are many blind ones seasoned in the embossing method. I admire the simplicity of your method, and I know more about it than you might think. People here have been reporting to me," he said significantly.

"But try to understand. You fail to comprehend the difficulties of administering a school in part endowed with public funds. We were able to get those funds after much maneuvering through ministries and after much intervention by highly placed people. Think you now of what would happen if at one blow everything we have maintained as being of value were suddenly to become valueless. Ministers would lose patience with us. We would have serious difficulties with finances.

"That is what you are up against with your new method and I tell you frankly that I will oppose you at every turn even to the point of recommending your dismissal. You see, I am being very frank," he concluded.

"But what shall I do with my method?" Braille asked unhappily. "What shall I do? Shall I discard it?"

"Do what you wish, my friend, but keep it out of this school and do not presume to use it officially in this school. Or, for that matter, unofficially. I do not wish to speak of this any more," he said, slapping the table vehemently.

For the next week Braille barely crept about his duties. His high elation and sense of destiny were crushed. He felt emptied, lonely, broken. He thought of returning to Coupvray; he felt the need of a mother's comfort. He was then twenty years old and a defeated man.

IX Blaze at Noon

SOON HE BEGAN TO COME OUT FROM UNDER HIS DARK-
ness and defeat. In a few weeks, he hired a private reader
who read to him selections from the various classics. As he
listened, he punched and punched on his little frame and
soon there was a great pile of manuscripts in his room.

He was the first blind man in history who dipped into
the wealth of the vast storehouse of literature. He was profoundly affected by what he read and reread in the night,
his fingers moving rapidly over glowing phrases and inspired
poetry.

He contacted musical friends and in the houses of the rich
he began to propagandize. He gave readings and followed

these with a short speech he had prepared. He tried to interest the rich and the great in his technique, but except for the smattering of applause which his readings and his little speech received, nothing concrete developed.

He did not know what he wished or what he sought to accomplish. He knew only that he must in some way gain the attention of the world—the seeing world.

"I am becoming a kind of buffoon," he told Denise, almost laughing at himself. "I give demonstrations in the drawing rooms of the great as though I were some kind of trickster, with a new kind of parlor game I have invented.

"The great ladies and gentlemen listen to me, watch me. Then there is a piano recital by someone, and they have had an evening of entertainment. After that, nothing happens. I am just another number on the evening's program. I wish I knew what to do . . ."

A highly placed friend, after much effort, finally got him a hearing before the Royal Institute.

He was very excited. "Now, I will have an official hearing. Now I will get universal recognition for my method," he shouted. "Everyone in the world listens to the Royal Institute. I will be given standing. I will show this is not just a parlor game."

Accompanied by Denise and attired in his best coat and wearing a lofty hat, he attended the session.

He sat on a bench at the side of a chemist who was about

to lecture on the properties of water. To his right, there was a balloon enthusiast who was sure, that given enough funds, he could cross the Channel to England by air.

On the platform a speaker was discoursing on the powers of the steam engine. A previous speaker had told of the new methods for combatting an insect which had devoured most of the French vines and thus ruined the wine industry that year.

The members of the Royal Institute themselves, all gray-beards, sat and stroked their faces, muttered to each other and paid scant attention to the men lecturing before them. To gain a hearing before the Royal Institute was then considered a signal honor. The Institute, first an honorary organization of men of science, had become a clearing house for new discoveries that were then flooding France along with the renaissance of invention.

Many of the Institute members were geniuses in science; but many too had obtained their posts through politics or through the intervention of influential friends or relatives.

A mumbling old man called Louis's name. He heard, sickeningly enough, the word "demonstration" being used in the account of what he was to show the Institute members.

He could hear no abatement in the buzz of conversation among the learned members on the rostrum before him. But he resolved to be his most commanding and to do his best. He prayed fervently to himself.

He had brought Denise to read for him, but he boldly discarded that plan and interrupted a burst of jovial laughter to ask that someone read to him.

"In this way," he said courteously to the assemblage, "there will be no suspicion of collusion. There will thus be no accusation that I have memorized a selection from anything."

The president of the Institute said sternly: "We are glad to accede to your request, Monsieur Braille. But understand it is not the custom of the Institute to have charlatans before it. We screen our lecturers in advance most devotedly for che sake of science."

Braille nodded humbly. "I am grateful for the opportunity to be heard," he said. "Messire, I wish to show only that the blind now have a simple, easy way with which to read and write. This is thanks to a miracle."

"Proceed, monsieur," the president said. An attendant began to read from a report that had been on the table in front of the president, on the coagulation of the blood. The report was replete with chemical formulas, but Braille punched and punched with a steady hand.

Denise, who was sitting in the well-like section of the lofty, round room, tore at her handkerchief nervously. Louis, from where she was sitting, was such a puny, pale, intense boy, his face lifted sightlessly, and his hands, like those of some acolyte at a devotion, working away at his now familiar frame.

The voice read and read, and Louis steadily punched away. The members still conversed among themselves and he could hear the impatient rustle from the other lecturers who were awaiting their turn on the bench below him.

He could hear the Institute members discussing a new dancer who was then the rage in Paris and then they turned to a spirited argument on the merits of some wine.

Of a sudden, he heard the president interrupt the banter and laughter: "That will do, Monsieur Braille. Please read to us now."

He reversed his thick sheets and his hands moved swiftly and with grace. Denise could see his knuckles standing up white against the thick foolscap with which he was working.

His tone was strong and measured. He stumbled at times over a German expression that had crept into the treatise on blood. But firmly, he continued while the president glanced idly at the original manuscript before him.

When he finished, he waited expectantly. But he heard only the old man voice the subject of the next lecturer on the session's program.

He dismounted from the platform, bowed in the direction of the president and his colleagues, and tapped his way out with Denise.

He was silent all the way home. He thanked Denise and said nothing. She sorrowed for him. Somehow, he felt de-flated. He did not know why.

If he expected anything from the hearing—and in some manner he had built up high hopes from being heard by the official Institute—he was doomed to disappointment.

A few weeks later, he received an official acknowledgment from the Royal Institute telling him that the French government thanked him for his efforts and his contribution to science.

And that was all.

Why he had expected more, he did not know. But he had felt that the hearing would be a turning point in his life and for his method. However, nothing happened. He felt flat and dull. He was melancholy; he felt aimless and uneasy. There seemed no horizons.

"I am a fool, I suppose. A great fool," he said to himself.

Now and then he had a classic read to him which he would "translate" into his cell notes. The solace of reading began to mean a great deal to him. He realized he was enjoying a pleasure that had been denied to every blind man since the creation of the world. "Even Baldar, the blind god, cannot do what I do," he told himself.

"I am the first blind man in history who can actually sit down and read something without any trouble, without a cumbersome technique. I can read as fast as anyone. Or at least almost as fast." Then his ego asserted itself: "I will be the most cultured blind man in history. That is something," and he smiled one of his rare smiles. "If I can pass this along to my blind brothers then I will be a very great man—one of the greatest of all time."

He sat at the window listening to the street sounds. Paris was bewitched that evening. He turned from his book and he felt the breeze on his face. He heard the voices of young people coming from church and his heart felt heavy. He longed for them and their companionship. He pictured himself talking and strolling with a young girl, kissing her, having her put her arm through his.

"What nonsense," he said out loud. "What girl would have me?" He heard gay laughter on the street and tried to form an image of the girl's face and it became the image of Denise as he thought she looked, and something inside of him melted.

With that, he heard Denise's step on the stairs. By this time, she had free access to the school building.

She came in, kissed him lightly on the cheek as she always did and for the first time in their long association he was disturbed by her presence. She flung her coat across a chair and nestled down on his bed humming a tune.

"Must you always be humming?" he asked irritably.

"You are in a bad mood today, my friend," she said quietly. "A very bad mood. Shall I go?"

"Go if you want to," he almost shouted. "Go. Go."

"What is wrong, Louis?" She was on her knees at his side. He burst into tears he could not account for. She stroked his hair and gathered his head to her bosom.

"Denise," he said. "Denise why are you so devoted to me? I am blind. I am nothing. Do you pity me?"

He took her in his arms and kissed her without realizing what he was doing. He felt her tremble and then she began to cry. It frightened him because she had never acted this way before. Also, it gave him a start to realize that she was a woman and not a child any longer.

"Louis, Louis. I have waited for this so long. Louis, you are so wonderful, so intelligent, so beautiful."

Seized by an impulse he could not understand he pushed her away. "You pity me. I can feel it. Go away. I never want to see you again." And he broke into mocking laughter. "I never want to *see* you again," he repeated. "What a farce. I will never see you. I am borrowing phrases from the books I read. It makes me feel almost normal and I am not normal."

She went to the window and looked out. "You are wrong, Louis. I love you. I want to be with you always. I can help you, care for you, work for you. I can be your eyes, your love, your heart. Don't be angry with me, Louis. I have waited for you for a long time."

He waited a moment. His senses were racing. He wanted desperately to believe her, but something within him resisted. His mind said one thing, his emotions another. He could not cope with the situation and in desperation he finally said, "If I had no money you would not care for me. Go away. Go away and leave me alone."

"You don't know what you are saying, Louis. You are up-set. I love you and I want to care for you always." Denise spoke very softly.

But Louis was bitter. "You are young. All young girls are impressionable and motherly."

"Louis, why are you bitter? It is not my fault that you are blind. Why do you blame me for it?" Then she became angry. "You don't know everything. You don't know about other people. You think the whole world revolves around blind people. You are very conceited and very intolerant. But you are wrong about me. I know I am being shameless when I tell you I love you. I don't love you because you are blind. I love you because you are you. Perhaps you will never understand that."

"I am sorry to upset you," he said, now contrite. "But I don't love you. I love only my work, my music, my teaching, my new cell method. We have nothing in common for I am a useless blind man and you are a normal young woman. You have a maternal feeling for me and I have no room in my life for any feeling at all. I may be conceited but I am not angry at you. I just want you to go away and forget all about me. Yours are just girlish dreams, that's all."

She put on her coat and stood in the doorway for a moment and asked in a small voice, "Must I go, Louis?"

"Yes, you must," he said. He heard her go out the door, heard it slam, then buried his face in his hands and cried. "I don't care," he said. But deep down he did care. He went out to the bistro and sat and sipped wine and all the while he felt an oppression that he could not overcome. He was emotionally undeveloped, and because he was immature and unworldly he did not realize that he was unwilling to face the fact that he had a fear of too close an association that might be disillusioning. Their contacts now were casual enough and she saw him always under favorable conditions. But marriage, that was confining; it might change his way of life. She might expect more of him than he was capable of giving. Besides, he was a dedicated person. He owed his life to all the unseeing. How could he desert them all for her? So he tortured himself with these hidden fears, which he did not recognize or understand, and built up a resistance within him. He flattered his ego by telling himself that he loved her, of course, but he could not inflict her life as his had been afflicted. And having made peace with his mind, he called himself an ass and decided to see her the next day.

But he behaved badly again. He acted like a martyr until Denise could stand it no longer. Never had he heard such ironical and callous laughter, as she threw back her head and shouted, "You are a fool. I used to respect you. But all you want to do is dramatize yourself. You think you are badly off. How about the one-legged veterans we see on the streets, those who fought with Napoleon in Russia? What about the men who had their eyes put out by bullets? How about those without any arms or legs? Paris is full of them. But you, you go around making a big fuss about the fact that you're blind. There are thousands of blind men in Paris, perhaps hundreds of thousands all over the world."

She pushed him toward the door. "Get out before I behave like a Paris fishwife. I am tired of your ego and your stupidity. You see nothing but yourself. You make my flesh crawl with your stupidity. Think on that, my friend," she said coldly. "Now go. I must meet a man in an hour. A real man. Not blind, either, if that will make you feel better."

"I did right," he said as he tapped up the street. "I certainly did right. I got her love for me out of her system. She will be happier now," he said righteously.

He even got nobler in his fancies. He said to himself: "I must have no woman around to distract me. I am dedicated to the blind. A woman would interfere with my work." And like many another tortured genius, he shook his head nobly, smiled a thin smile, the man of destiny, and went about his work. But the nights were very bad and occasionally he found himself humming the silly tunes Denise used to hum, and thinking of her sweet, gentle nature.

He plunged deeper into his work at the school and his organ recitals. It was at this point that he mastered the violoncello and involuntarily wrote and dedicated a sonata to Denise called "Youth is Spring—You are Spring."

Three months after the emotional storms with Denise, he received a short letter from her that she was married and living in Lyons.

"I hope you will be happy, Louis. I am writing this with the permission of my husband. When we come to Paris, we will come to see you. I read about your concerts in the papers and I am very proud of you. My very best wishes."

He did not answer. When the letter was read to him he knew what a fool he had been to let her go. He consoled himself by saying: "She will not be happy without me. She probably married an imbecile." But the words in her letter were well remembered and he repeated them often to himself.

It was perhaps the worst period of his life. Worse than when he had fled the school and slept on sacks in the fruiterer's shop; worse than when he had been spanked by Haüy; worse even than when he had first lost his eyesight.

After a while, he began to realize how foolish he had been and he did not torture himself so much. He grew calmer and graver and while he flattered himself for not having married her simply because of *his* deficiency, he was aware of a great grief because he had not done so.

"Maybe it is better so," he said philosophically. It was not better so and he knew it but talking himself out of it helped.

At one of the salons he frequented, he had another opportunity to find love and comfort and again rejected it because of a willful and false pride.

The Countess Lafiche, of a noble French family, widowed at the age of twenty-two when her husband was killed in the battle of Austerlitz, was of a very romantic nature and very rich. History says that Marianne was not very beautiful, but of course Louis did not know that. He knew only her rich voice, a throaty contralto, and he knew too her very comfortable carriage in which she would transport him home to the school.

One night, when she was taking him home she leaned forward and kissed his palm. He was astounded and at the same time incensed. "Why do you do that?" he asked coldly.

"You play very beautifully. I love music and you are a very handsome man," she said pertly.

"There is no room for women in my life," he said sharply. "I have things to do."

"That's what makes you so attractive," Marianne said winningly.

She pursued him for several weeks and then when he repulsed her for the last time, she slapped him, put him out of her carriage and shouted: "You are a fool. Perhaps you think you are a god. Well, monsieur, there is only one God."

He took her hand, lifted it to his lips, and said ironically: "Try and forget me. It will be difficult, I know, but try." He heard an unladylike remark, and she told her coachman to drive on.

Shortly thereafter a pupil of his also fell in love with him and he behaved again like a man of destiny who had no time in his life for frivolities. "Georgette," he said, "there is no room in my life for happiness. I must plunge forward with my music, with my reading system. You will understand, I know."

Louis was never again to know the companionship of a woman or her love. As time went on, he avoided them more and more. He missed the companionship of Denise and was often lonely and bitter. He wondered what attitude to take toward her when she visited Paris, but he was spared the agony, for she never came and he stopped hoping.

X Another Dusk

ONE DAY, ONE OF HIS STUDENTS WAS IN HIS ROOM DIS-
cussing an event of the day. Braille asked him whether he
would like to be read to.

The lad, with some embarrassment, blurted out, "I have
heard of your reading method, sir. They all laugh at it."

Braille said nothing, though he was deeply wounded. He
took a thick, loosely bound manuscript from his great store
in his closet, and read from his own punchings. It was from
Shakespeare.

The boy was enthralled. Secretly, he began to come to
Braille's room and soon was joined by others in the school.
There began for Braille a double life.

During the day, at his classes, he taught the traditional

embossing method. At night, there would steal to his room more than a dozen students to whom he taught his cell method of dots.

In a few months, he had an entire class, an unscheduled class, of devotees who worshipped him. He was never so happy, even with his music.

"Look," he would exclaim happily. "We have a class in writing, we blind ones. We can write each other if we wish."

The students learned to keep their bodkins and frames within their shirts and now and then would pass notes to each other.

One of these was seized in the classroom and an instructor, jealous of Braille, turned it in to La Porte.

Braille was called in. "You need not ask why you are here," the director said. "I warned you a long time ago and you still persist. There will be no more infractions, no more night classes. Is that clear?"

Braille stood his ground. "You cannot defeat the march of science, monsieur. You cannot keep the blind from reaching out. If my method died, a new one would be devised by another. Of this, I am sure. However, I acquiesce in what you say simply because I do not wish my students to have trouble with you.

"I will tell you this," he said defiantly and with great emotion. "My night-time students have learned more in a few months than the Institute can teach them in years. I have given them more in a few months than they would have acquired at your school studying all of their lives. Understand that.

"My students can write to each other!" he shouted with fury, banging on La Porte's desk with his cane. "Can yours do the same? Can they, can they?" he yelled.

But it was of no use and Louis ceased his night classes.

Cheerlessly, he continued to live at the Institute, made his way to the church organ, taught some few blind to play, and gave an infrequent recital on the violoncello, which was always well attended.

His financial problems were few. He had no friends he particularly cared about except some few with whom he would talk music. Rarely did he mention his method but he thought of it constantly with anguish. He was inconsolable because it had not caught on, that it had not come to flower.

"I am practically the only blind man in the world who can read and write. I am thus the loneliest man in the world," he said to himself despondently, pacing his room in the Paris wintertime. Outside, he could hear the cheerful sleigh bells, the shouts of children. He was alone, terribly alone.

"I am even lonelier than before I invented my system," he thought. "Then, at least, I was excited about the possibility. Today, I have not even that hope for tomorrow."

His sole comfort came from his reading, from the books he himself had transcribed from the readings given him by the man he had hired.

In 1839, his address before the Royal Institute was published and he received many letters from similar workers throughout the world, from men who were trying to improve the lot of the blind.

Interestingly enough, and amazing to him, was the fact that most of the workers in a new language for the blind were merely seeking a way to embellish the embossing method. Braille, apparently, stood alone, and he often wondered whether he were not off the beaten track.

"But how can I be wrong?" he argued to himself. "I write and read with books that are far from cumbersome. Compare my method with the embossing system. I can read faster. I can read more clearly. I do not hold a mountain in my lap when I am reading. Best of all, and most important, I can write. I cannot understand why it has not caught on, this poor orphan invention of mine. No one loves it."

There was nothing wrong with the Braille method as the world was to discover. He, alone with many discoverers, was suffering from late recognition, from a lack of what we know today as "press-agentry." There was just no one to spread his "dot" method abroad, to make it available and sought-after.

Like many a painter or poet who has been "discovered" after death, Braille was to know the bitterness of nonrecognition. And the bitterness had a sharp, biting edge to it that left him sick and furious.

But happily enough and in contrast to the lives of scores of other unappreciated geniuses, one high moment was to come in his lifetime. The moment was to have a movie-like quality. But come it did, and happily enough, from his music.

Among the pupils to whom he taught the organ and the violoncello, was a young, lovely blind girl by the name of Therese von Kleinert, of Alsace-Lorraine extraction.

This young girl showed a great enthusiasm for the organ, at the time mainly an instrument for men. But she leaned more toward the piano, a somewhat different instrument today from what it was then, one hundred years ago.

Her talent was remarkable, and her grace and beauty of such piquant quality that she soon became a frequent visitor at the same salons Braille visited, rarely of late, because of his more accentuated cough and his increased bitterness.

Braille, early in their association at the church where he had the use of the organ, instructed her in the dot method. She speedily caught on, and with Louis's help soon set up a musical library all written in the Braille system. She used these whenever she performed in concert.

In 1841, she was asked to perform at a concert at the fashionable salon of Madame Desmoulins, a widow with a vast fortune who attracted the cream of Paris culture and wit.

Braille had been scheduled to play the violoncello, but was unable to be present because of illness. His cough had turned tubercular and he was failing rapidly.

The young girl tapped her way to the piano with the cautious gait that was rendered the more touching because of her youth and beauty.

She clutched under her arm her sheaf of music, about a foot thick and all rendered into Braille's cell system.

She turned as she touched the piano and curtsied to the glittering assemblage. There were writers, artists, journalists, military men, diplomats—the intellectuals of Paris.

The young girl leaned into her work. She played without touching a note on the thick sheets before her.

Now and then, she would flash a hand and scan the sheets with her fingers, in pauses, and riffle over them.

She played stormily and tenderly and her final selection was a tinkling, gentle note of Braille's own composition.

The applause was tremendous.

She stood gracefully at the side of the piano, acknowledging the applause which rose in fervor. Then she held up a hand for silence.

She stepped forward and, her blind face seeking the audience, she said: "Mesdames et messieurs, it is not I who play tonight but rather a broken, bewildered and dying man. Many of you know of Louis Braille, the great organist, but few of you know of him as a giver of light—as I do. Most of you acclaim him as a musician, but none of you know of him as a seeker of truth in his darkness—as I do."

There was a silence, and she continued:

"He is dying today of tuberculosis. But he is dying the

more rapidly because of frustrations. Not because, as a blind man he has not achieved a great measure of fame, as you know, at the organ. But the more because he has pierced the shadows across the eyes of the blind, and he cannot reach across to them.

"Tonight, I have been able to play only because of Braille's teaching. Without his teaching, I could not play so readily. Without his teaching, I would be almost an animal in my blindness.

"I beg of you, then, to applaud the dying man who is not here, and not to applaud me. I play through his eyes."

The simple statement by the simple girl was caught up by the sophisticated throng. The following day, the Paris news-papers were full of Braille and of the young girl. What usual and logical channels had failed to achieve, a clever piece of press-agentry, as we know it now, won the day.

In a few months, so much did the tale touch the hearts of the impressionable Parisians that a citizen's committee was formed to conduct an investigation. The report published by the Royal Institute was dug up and reprinted. Several of the newspapers used the occasion to attack the directors of the Institute whom they called "doddering, aged and useless in a world of science."

The directors of the Royal Institute hastened to rectify its standing and petitioned the government for a grant for Braille so that he might pursue what they called "meritorious research." Unfortunately, however, the stipend, amounting to about $200 annually, was refused by Louis because his work was to be under the "guidance and direction of the Royal Institute."

He told the directors of the Institute, in a very strong letter, that he did not feel himself bound to submit to anyone's direction. "Unless I have a free hand," he wrote, "I will not continue except on my own. Why should I do all the work and have you worthy gentlemen claim the credit later as you have done on many previous occasions?"

Whether he was wrong or right, no one can tell. His rejection of the income fund was regarded unfavorably and one newspaper hinted that "perhaps M. Braille is too proud and too egotistical. After all, it has not yet been established that his method is the best. There are other reading methods for the blind." The newspaper then went on to describe the Fry method, which a Dr. Fry of London had developed and for which he had received a prize of $100 given by the Scottish Society of Arts. Louis was familiar with the Fry system and also with that devised by James Gall, of Edinburgh, in 1827.

However, Louis had discounted these simply because they were based on variations of the alphabet and did not allow for fast reading. Moreover, he considered them useless because it was expensive to put out books based on raised lettering.

The human-interest furor which had been raised by the Braille story soon subsided in face of other things. Louis

Napoleon, the President of France, was attempting to restore France as a monarchy with himself as emperor and newspapers in France were hard put to maintain their independence. They were fighting Louis Napoleon's efforts to license them and place them under government control. Louis was forgotten in the hurly-burly of a France which was undergoing great changes in its national life because of a would-be emperor.

He became dispirited, moodier than ever, and only when a new piece of music came his way, did he perk up. In Germany and Vienna some of the greatest compositions that the world was to know were being written and performed at that time, and many of them made their way, after a while, to Paris.

But even music soon left him shrugging his shoulders with impatience. His following among pupils dropped off as he became more and more embittered. And he was rarely invited out to salons any more.

But his early bitterness soon wore off when he found to his consternation that his friends were avoiding him. "Have I become a bore?" he asked himself and he was seasoned and sophisticated enough to realize that he had become one. "Apparently all I talk about is my reading system, and the worst thing a Frenchman can be accused of is that of being a bore," he told himself with a wry smile.

So, very much like many another genius before and after him, he developed the inimitable custom of shrugging his shoulders. His face took on a kindlier look than it had for a long time and he fell into a frame of thinking that was healthy for him. "Perhaps my system is wrong. I can't be right if the world pays me no attention. After all, I may be biased," he said with a rueful smile.

But beneath it all, his heart was breaking with defeat and his cough became worse. He resigned himself to dreaming of Denise and he developed a particular affection for the children who lived next door at the tailoring shop. From his funds, he bought them toys and he amused them by letting them climb on his back.

He was very gray though he was still young. He spent most of his last days at the sidewalk cafés listening to the music of voices and of footsteps and to the sound of the carriages on the boulevards. At times he dreamed of translating all of the poets into his reading system but his energies were not up to it.

In 1851 he left the Institute and, with a small store of money he had saved, he took a tiny room in a garret. He never played the violoncello or the organ again simply because the exercise moved him to an emotion he could not control and that left him racking with cough. He was then forty-one years old.

He made friends with the revolutionaries of Germany who had fled their country in 1848 and who had flocked to Paris. He told them of his system and he was happy when they told him that he too was a revolutionary against the bad order of things.

Now and then he went to church to hear the organ music and then he found himself becoming intensely religious. Unconsciously, he seemed to know that death was near and he shed himself of anger and pride and his impatience with what he called "stupidity." His face, because of the blind eyes and the tired smile and the gray hair, was a beautiful sight and he was vastly amused when one of his new friends from Germany, a painter, asked him to pose for an allegory he was doing on history.

"What do you want me to pose for you as?" he asked good-naturedly.

"As God, monsieur," the painter said. "For God is blind even as you are and your face is closer to my impression of God than anyone I have ever seen."

Louis smiled tiredly. "I don't believe God is blind, my friend," he said. "My notion of Him is not yours. I will not lend myself to your bitterness."

But when in March of 1852 he took to his bed in his garret, for once he knew fear.

"I will die and my system will die with me," he thought feverishly. He called his landlady and begged her to summon his friends.

Three of them, one a journalist, another a composer, and a third a shopkeeper, came to see him.

"I am very tired," he told them. "Please, please, if my system for the blind is of any merit, I don't want it to be lost. Please help me and please help my blind friends."

Then he settled half of his funds on his landlady who had been so kind to him and the rest on needy students at the Institute. There wasn't much more for him to do.

He was alone in his tiny room on March 28th when he died. His end was not known until a day later when his landlady came up to see why she hadn't heard him coughing.

The Paris newspapers carried a very small story, perhaps a paragraph, and he was forgotten almost immediately. No one of particular note attended his funeral, but according to the meager records kept of the time the day was very sunny.

It was not until 1854, two years after his death, that official recognition came to him. And it was brought about indirectly by himself. The blind giant had labored even better than he knew. Therese von Kleinert, the young musician whom he had taught, gave a series of concerts which attracted the attention of Louis Napoleon, who by then had become emperor.

Louis Napoleon was then planning for the Paris International Exposition, which was scheduled for the following year. He granted an audience to the accomplished blind girl and ordered that the Braille system be included in the exposition's exhibits. The emperor had planned the great event to show how France had developed culturally, economically and scientifically under his benign hand.

He thought it would be a good stunt for Therese to be stationed at the exposition and show how a blind person can play the piano under a system invented by a Frenchman.

It worked and worked rapidly. Visitors were tremendously impressed with the novelty and brought word back to almost every country in Europe.

From that point on, Braille's genius opened windows to the blind all over the world, in every climate and in every tongue wherever the tap of the cane was heard.

Except for the Moon system, one that uses raised lines in the forms of angles and curves and is more easily learned by those who are blinded later in life, Braille's method is the standard the world over.

There is hardly a government, even in the backward areas of the Far East and the Middle East, that does not encourage, with funds and schools, the teaching of the blind with Louis's method. There is no nation that does not have at least one organization devoted to Braille. His name, in most dictionaries, in most languages, is not even spelled with a capital "B," but refers to the word as a system rather than a man.

The blind today are barred, because of their deficiency, from very, very few occupations. They can vie at colleges and at many factories with the seeing.

Louis's revered sponsor, Valentin Haüy, has since been given the title "Father and Apostle of the Blind." Louis is regarded, wherever civilized men meet, as the son.

Could he see today what he wrought, the busy workshops, the libraries and the schools and the musicians—peopled by the blind—he would bang a table with his cane and shout with excitement and pleasure. Perhaps he is.

strates system at Royal Academy, 127-130; becomes convinced Denise pities him, 132-134; Denise tells him to leave, 135, 136; dedicates a sonata to Denise, 136; meets Countess Lafiche, 137; leaves the Countess, 138; meets and is loved by Georgette, 138; teaches the Braille system secretly, 139-140; La Porte orders him to stop, 140, 141; address before Royal Institute published, 142; becomes tubercular, 144, 145; Royal Institute address reprinted, 145; rejects grant from the Institute, 145, 146; plays with neighborhood children, 148; is asked to pose in allegory, 149; dies, 150; Napoleon orders Braille system exhibited, 150

BRAILLE, (SR.) LOUIS
saddle-maker, 13, 14; makes toys for son, 14; named to village council, 15; raises funds for new bell, 15; promises

reins to advocate, 15; finds son has injured his eye, 17 takes son to local veterinarian, 18; takes son to Paris for examination, 19; is told left eye is gone, 20; is told right eye may be affected, 21; blames self for son's injury, 21; makes cane for son, 23; takes son to school, 25; agrees that son may go to Haüy's school, 38; offers to pay tuition of others, 41; receives letter from son, 46; comes to take son home, 46; son decides to stay at school, 46, 47; sends son alphabet in leather, 48; welcomes son's return, 68; dies, 71

BRAILLE "SYSTEM"
"cell" system discovered, 118; system described, 119, 120; perfected, 121; demonstrated by Louis, 122, 123, 127-130; taught secretly, 139-141; publicized, 144, 145, 150, 151

About the Author

J. ALVIN KUGELMASS was born in
New York City, attended Townsend
Harris High, City College, Columbia
University and the New School for Social Research. He started his newspaper
career while still in college, and has been
on the staffs of various newspapers across
the country. He has also been a corres-
pondent for the major news services, has
contributed to leading national maga-
zines, and is the author of several biog-
raphies for young people. Mr. Kugelmass
and his family now live in San Jose,
California.

DATE DUE

GAYLORD   #3523PI   Printed in USA